South East
# Asian
## COOKING

# South East Asian COOKING

## TINO ROZZO

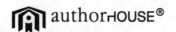

*AuthorHouse™ LLC*
*1663 Liberty Drive*
*Bloomington, IN 47403*
*www.authorhouse.com*
*Phone: 1-800-839-8640*

*Published by AuthorHouse    02/25/2014*

*ISBN: 978-1-4918-6778-5 (sc)*
*ISBN: 978-1-4918-6779-2 (e)*

*Library of Congress Control Number: 2014904022*

# CONTENTS

# THAILAND

## MYANMAR (BURMA)

## BHUTAN
## (Land of the Thunder Dragon)

# CAMBODIA

# TIBET

# MONGOLIA

# VIETNAM

# MAYLASIA

# INTRODUCTION

It is not easy to write a cookbook. Providing recipes is a lot of work and only an experienced cook, professional Chef or not, would know if a recipe works or not.

When I started cooking Asian foods, I was living on my own. Luckily I had a Chinatown ear by and Asian grocers offered bargains on food and condiments.

It was not long when I started to take menus from restaurants I could not afford and started cooking in my apartment kitchen. A refrigerator stove, sink combo with two burners.

I bought a Wok at the Mall, and a small sauce pan. For a long time in my tiny apartment I made some really wonderful Asian recipes. It isn't hard to hack a recipe off a menu. The public library offered sources on the way these cuisines could be made. Spending much time in Asian markets and getting to know the condiments, I would even at time, freelance a recipe and make something of my own.

It is easy to see that many recipes one could make can replicate already existing traditional recipes. If one studies the ways and means, one can get the notion of how things are done.

I was accustomed to New York's Chinatown. My parents used to visit Little Italy and right here across Canal Street, is Chinatown. Visiting that part of New York made me feel as though I was especially in a movie. I loved hearing the Asian music and the wonders of that section of New York. What a marvel in my mind two great historic cultures living right across the street from each other. My cultural ground zero and attribute to being an American is that Mulberry St. and Canal St is my cultural center in life.

New York's Chinatown has grown amazingly. It is now many times larger than Little Italy. Greenwich Village offers a great Italian neighborhood, but that is for another book.

As life journey continued I found myself in Philadelphia. Philly has grown in years. Chinatown found itself behind the Gallery Mall. I have frequently traveled to this Chinatown and discovered many Asian wonders. In years my travels to South Street's Italian Market has lead to the development of the Vietnamese Market. Nice, another Asian society, Another American miracle! It seems the Italian American Community welcomed the Vietnamese because Italian Americans remember their immigrant struggles. There are some great markets and Vietnamese stores that are recommended to visit.

There have been many Vietnamese markets with in the South Street Market, but this current development is awesome.

Vietnamese restaurants offer great lunch special bargains. And I recommend them. One of my favorite is called the Buddhist Hot Pot. Sometimes it goes by another name. It has meat, tofu, pineapples, and a Asian cucumber called beiheh. It is served in a stainless steel pot with a flame under it.

There is a future for a Vietnamese cookbook. But I want it to be special and out of the ordinary. There are already a few really good Vietnamese cookbooks in print.

Cherry Hill NJ has developed a really nice Asian area. There are now Vietnamese and Korean markets along the main routes. There are some very good opportunities to explore.

Cherry Hill in years has really developed a great international restaurants. It can be called the Culinary Capital of the Delaware Valley.

It seems Asian communities are growing in the USA also. In Fort Lee NJ, and Cliffside Park NJ there are developments of Asian variety. Fort Lee has a Koreatown now, and

New York City has a good Koreatown in the center of Manhattan.

Of course there are other Asians varieties such as Indian and Thai food. II discovered Indian food at a restaurant in Fair Lawn NJ. I had my first South East Asian adventures there.

Thusly, I discovered Thai in the Bronx one day when I visited a Chinese Astrologer. Unfortunately none of her predictions came true. I never had enough money for extravagant travel. Luckily in America, even with "Low Dough" (meaning people short on funds). We can experience

Something different and unique that is not available in many countries. But Thai, Indian, and Vietnamese where not the only food adventures one could have. New York's Asian population grew incredibly now serving a wide variety of Asian cuisines. One of my new favorites is Burmese. The cuisine of Myanmar. Also, Malay has become a new entry in the Asian food experience. North Jersey and New York have become a food paradise for the world.

For people in Los Angles and San Francisco, Asian cuisine has probably been more available before reaching the East Coast. Too some extant that is true.

One day I met a friend named Allan Kehler. He was from Ashland, Pennsylvania. He used to come to New Jersey to visit me from a very long way. Allan's family had a business and Allan became available to travel. Our first trip was to Hawaii. We stayed at the Rainbow Hilton in Waikiki. As we toured Honolulu and other sites on the Island. Although Hawaii claims its own cuisine, obviously heavily based in Asian cuisine, there was a vast variety of Asian foods to try. Allan became my sponsor in many adventures. Many of his friends could not get past greasy spoon establishments.

Maui had a lot to offer. From the time we landed, we saw Pineapple Farms and many local products. Lahaina is a quaint village with many Asian Restaurants. We visited a friend from New York, Satomi Seki, wife of Reverend Hozen Seki. Sensei Seki was the founder of the New York Buddhist Church. He had two sons Hoken, of Lake Forest, Ill., and Hoshin, of Mount Vernon, N.Y.

I still see Hoshin from time to time at New York and New Jersey O-Bon festivals.

When I was young there was a Restaurant in Fair Lawn NJ called Chan's Hawaiian Islander. They had a Tiki cocktail named The Flaming Virgin. In Hawaii, they never heard of it. The Cocktail came in a Tiki cup and of course a it is a flaming drink.

One waiter made fun of me when I asked about the Flaming Virgin, "That is New Jersey Hawaiian". Allan and I took our next vacation to San Francisco. In San Francisco there was another great discovery. I was seeking the Italian Neighborhood, which is called North Beach. South Across Broadway is Chinatown. Two Cities with an Italian and Chinese neighborhood North and South of each other.

And yes, varied Asian restaurants.

Outside Chinatown though we found a excellent Cambodian Restaurant. A new discovery from another Asian culture. Right here in America we can see and taste the world in our own back yard. I always surmised that. As a kid I visited the iron Bound Section of Newark NJ where they have a Portuguese and Brazilian neighborhood.

In Paterson NJ we have many Puerto Ricans, Cubans, and South Americans. John Lennon was right when he said the whole world converges on New York. I am not taking anything away from San Francisco. We on the East had Ellis Island, in San Francisco they had Angle Island. As Europeans came through Ellis Island, Asian came through Angle Island.

San Francisco's Chinatown , and North Beach are not on flat land. North Beach looks more Italian than most Little Italy's in America. San Francisco's Chinatown looks like a living movie set.

Me and Allan felt like a couple of Marco Polo's discovering new cultures. And we where able to have some fun with some of the locals. The people we met gave us a lot of joy. I can still remember after all these years what we had to eat and the recipes I hacked.

Allan enjoyed my tour guide efforts being savvy to New York, and Philly's Chinatown. In San Francisco we used the yellow pages to plot our next adventures.

No book or groups of pictures can give the feeling of being there. With the magic of the internet we can go to video sights and have a glimpse of what we are interested in. When we where not traveling I would cook for Allan after his long journey. I'd whip out the Wok and conjure up an Asian meal.

Unfortunately, as time passed, After we returned from our San Francisco trip Allan passed away on January 10th 1995. I lost a friend, Buddy, and eating partner. If it where not for Allen this book would not be possible. Being Pure Land Buddhists when Allen and I experienced profound gratitude we would say "Namo Amida Butsu." "Awe place our faith in the Buddha of infinite light and life."

This book is for all the Allen Kehler's (Marco Polo's) out there in foody land.

Read about Chinatown's online at: http://chinatownhi.techmonde. net/?q=node/4

Remember not all Asian cultures are alike. Although The Chinese have a great influence, like the west the Greeks and Romans have a major influence in the West.

The culture of Asia has varied civilizations in Asia. It features different kinds of cultural heritage of many regions, societies, and ethnic groups

Asian art, music, and cuisine, Cinema and literature, are important parts of each nations culture culture. Eastern philosophy and religions and religions also plays a major role in development, Hinduism, Taoism, Confucianism, Buddhism, and Islam all playing major roles.

Unlike North East Asian, South East Asia has there own Architecture, Agriculture, and ecological factors differing from other parts of Asia.

Linguistic differences, minority groups, ethnic subcultures, and nationality each take on a uniqueness. A common thread with many other elements of the Earth.

Although I have included Tibet and India, these are near South East Asian countries. Mongolia is not South East either, yet, The Asian cultural stamp is important. Looking at Mongolian cuisine is related to China and Russia, but seeable more Chinese. Though Mongols do not seem to use Sesame Oil and Soy Sauce as the Chinese do. The Mongolian Hot Pot and other dishes are told to be Mongolian have no authenticity. It is next to impossible to find a mongol Restaurant in the USA, but Tibetan cuisine maybe more available in some towns.

Generally Mongol Cuisine contains a lot of Mutton. I'd like to thank Buyanzaya for her insights as we spoke much about Mongol Cuisine. And many who with the magic of electronic communication gave me their recipes.

# EXOTIC FOODS

There is a long standing argument about whether we should consume exotic foods. Some say we should not eat exotic, others believe there is no harm.

My view is what is exotic? When I grew up In Paterson NJ, there where many immigrant cultures and societies in the area. I Eaten Chinese, which to me was common since we had many Chinese establishments in town. Any Hispanics are in New Jersey and New York. No one needed a restaurant to try that those cuisines.

Everything from Puerto Rican to Brazilian was available.

There was Indian, Thai, Japanese, Korean, and other eating opportunities to try something new was available.

Andres Zimmern has gone around the world trying bizarre foods. But then again he seems to be sampling what the local people eat, and yet his new shows have focused on America.

Tony Bourdain has traveled around the world getting stoned on the local hootch and sampling native and American foods.

The three of us have been to Sardinia and I Eat Sardinian food regularly. Some people have accused me of exotic eating. Italian and Sardinian are common for me.

If you have neighbors who are Indian, Thai, Indonesian, or what ever, they are not going to think there food is exotic.

The problem of exotic is when people are exploiting rare and endangered animals.

But now people have found the Global Village is coming to them America is the original Global Village and its birth place, OK, Canada too.

And in the Holistic Health Industry, exotic plants and juices are distributed for people who are into preventative, organic health practices.

I found in a pinch, when cooking South East Asian, I can get some of the tropical ingredients in Spanish markets.

Coconut, Chyotes, spices.

Curry is a sauce and mixed spice (Garam Masala) in South East Asia. Eating foods that are prepared with turmeric or curry can help prevent atherosclerosis, some types of cancer and Alzheimer's disease. It can decrease pain and stiffness related to rheumatoid arthritis and osteoarthritis. It reduces indigestion and can aid in digestive disorders such as easing the discomfort of inflammatory bowel disease and irritable bowel syndrome.

Here is some information of the holistic effects of some herbs and spices.

**Turmeric**
Contains curcumin, which can inhibit the growth of cancer cells.

**Cumin**
This spice is extremely good for digestion and digestive problems., the main component of its essential oil, activates our salivary glands oral cavity, which facilitates the essential digestion.

**Rosemary**
Stops gene mutations that could lead to cancer and may help prevent damage to the blood vessels that raise a possible heart attack.

**Garlic**
Destroys cancer cells and often disrupts the metabolism of tumor cells.

**Paprika**
It's content contains capsaicin, an anti-inflammatory and antioxidant. The effects may lower the risk of cancer this is also found in cayenne and red chili peppers.

**Ginger**
Decrease motion sickness and nausea; may also relieve pain and swelling caused by arthritis. Asians some times may even put this is a confection, I once found round ginger candy balls.

**Oregano**
This herb has the highest antioxidant activity of 27 fresh culinary herbs.

**Cinnamon**
Prevents type-2 diabetes and heart disease. Because of cinnamon's affect on blood sugar.

**Basil (Varieties:Sweet and Lemmon)**
One of the primary medicinal uses of basil comes from(E)-beta-caryophyllene, a natural anti-inflammatory compound. It has much in common with oregano and medicinal cannabis.

**Cilantro**
This is most often seen as being effective for toxic metal cleansing, this herb is a powerful, natural cleansing compound. The chemical compounds in cilantro bind to toxic metals and loosen them from the tissues.

**Lemongrass**
Inhibits microbial and bacterial growth in the body, both internally and externally, helping to prevent and cure bacterial infections, respiratory system, urinary tract, stomach, colon.

With the exotic label added and moralists preaching exotic food are bad for us should take a second look. Also, before Jacque Cousteau passed away he mentioned that the agricultural base in South and

Central American Rain Forests have the possibility of new cures for many diseases.

Jacques Cousteau: *Sometimes we are lucky enough to know that our lives have been changed, to discard the old, embrace the new, and turn headlong down an immutable course.*

And

*The awareness of our environment came progressively in all countries with different outlets.*

So you see. We are all interrelated and interdependent on the Earth, the environment, and fellow human beings. The art, music, food, and culture make life a joy and are healthy for us. We must exercise discretion on dietary planning. Life is meant to be lived and enjoyed. I heard the quote.

*"Cuisine is man kind's immediate access to civilized culture."*
The world is one human family and in the kindness and generosity we embraces means that we are truly human. If we had children around the world in various places, we would love all of them because they are part of us.

# INDIA

# Garam Marsala

This is the basic curry powder of India and South East Asia. This is used frequently.

Cardamom
Cumin
Turmeric
Fenugreek
Coriander
Black pepper
Red pepper
Cloves (crushed)
Bay leaf (crushed)
Pimento

1. If you are making a basic recipe on tbsp. of each in a small container.
2. If you wish to make a container measure ingredients. from 2 to 4 ounces.

# Curry sauce

3/4 cup chicken stock
3/4 cup cream
3/4 cup coconut milk
1/2 cup of ghee
2 tbsp flour
2 tsp. garam masala
1 tbsp lemon juice
1 tsp. turmeric
1 tsp. cumin

1.  Make a rue of the flour and ghee by melting the ghee in A wok
    or pan and spread it all around. Add the flour and stir till it is
    a hazel nut color. Don't let it brown or burn.
2.  Add the stock, cream, and milk. Let it heat till it thickens and
    simmers. Do not boil it. It should be cooked on moderate heat.
3.  Add all the spices and lemon juice, integrate well.

*   The milk cream can be eliminated and a heavy coconut cream
could be used in conjunction with a light coconut cream. One
recipe called for a egg yellow mixed into the cream before adding
it to the pan. Do so if you wish

–

# Appetizers

## Samosas

Through out my travels, this has become one of my favorites. The meat used here in this recipe is called Keema. This can be a dish in itself.

1 lb ground lamb
2 onions (skinned and sliced)
4 cloves of garlic (crushed)
2 tsp. of Chili powder
1 tsp. Turmeric
1/4 cup of coriander
1 tsp. cumin
Pinch of salt
1/4 cup of ghee

1.  Melt ghee in a pan and fry the onions and garlic until the onions are translucent.
2.  Add lamb and spices and stir-fry till the meat is done.

The pastry dough.

Either use Spanish pasty discs, or make your own pastry dough. This can be stuffed into a puff pastry with almost the same method.

For discs: Cut circle in half, fill halves with Keema, then seal the edges. You can leave the pastry discs whole if desired. Puff pastry: 2 cups of flour, cold water and 3/4 cups of butter. Beat these in a food processor till they are smooth. Put them into the refrigerator for two hours. Then roll them out to 2« inches in diameter and stuff them with Keema. Heat the oven to 375o and bake 30 minutes or till the puff pastry is golden brown.

\*   Vegetarians can substitute lame with potatoes and green peas.

# Pakoras

This is a batter for vegetables as tempora. Many cultures have a fritter recipe and this is India contribution.

I cup of Chick pea flour (Besan)
1 tsp. ginger
2/3 cup of plain yogurt
1 tsp. of lemon juice
Vegetables of choice(Egg plant, squash, carrots, etc.)

1.  Sift the flour in a bowl and make sure all the flour is not clumped or lumped. Sieve it if need be.
2.  Add the chili powder and a pinch of salt, mix it well.
3.  Add the lemon juices, then yogurt gradually. Beat it well.

Leave it for two hours. This batter will be thicker then most, it can be loosened if need be wit a little milk.

4.  Heat a deep fryer or pan to 370o F. Dip each vegetable piece in the batter and place in the basket and lower it in the oil. It will be easy to tell when these are cooked.

*   Make sure the vegetables are thinly sliced. Meat such as chicken and shrimp, and lamb is suggested.
Panir is a India cheese shaped into a ball, Panir Pakora can be made by dipping the cheese balls in the batter and deep-fried.

# Channe Chi Chat

Chickpeas
Tomatoes
Potatoes
chopped onions
2 cloves of garlic (minced)
2 tsp. ginger (Sliced or grated)
1 tsp. sugar (Neutralizes tamarind bitterness)
1/4 to 1/2 cup of tamarind juice
India black salt

1.  Cook chick peas and potatoes, leave the onions and tomatoes raw.
2.  Add a little oil to a frying pan, fry the garlic and ginger. Add the sugar and tamarind. Cook for 1 minute.
3.  Place the vegetables in a bowl, add the sauce and toss. Top it with India black salt.

*   This is a dish best served cold.

—

# India Style Dip-(Similar too Greek Tzatsiki.)

1 1/4 cup of plain yogurt
1 tsp. cumin
1/2 tsp. chili powder
1 tsp. grated ginger
pinch of sea salt
mint leaves or coriander (both if you wish)
1/2 cucumber (grated or finely chopped

Place all these in a mixer or food processor for a minute
or two. Serve cold.

# Tikka (Kabobs)

1 lb of meat chunks
4 onions (quartered)
1 pepper (1 inch cubes)
3 garlic cloves (minced)
1 tsp. turmeric
1 tbsp vinegar
1 tbsp lemon juice
1 tsp. paprika
1 tsp. chili powder
3/4 cup or more of yogurt

1. Cut the meat in to 1 inch cubes, place them in a bowl and spoon on lemon juice.
2. Place the yogurt, spices, vinegar, and garlic in a food processor and mix well. Pour it over the meat and allow it to marinade over night.
3. With the remaining onions, and peppers, and meat of choice intermittently thread them on a skewer.
4. Place them on a grill or in the oven, 470oF, till cooked.

# Breads

## Chapatti

1. Whole wheat flour (Ata or Chapatti flour)
1 tsp. of salt
1 cup of water

1. Run flour through a sifter and make sure there are no lumps.
2. Add salt and lowly mix in the water making the dough.
3. Place extra flour on the board or table so the dough doesn't stick and kneed it.
4. Break the dough into 8 to 10 balls. Flatten them out thin. Use a tortilla press if one is handy. A rolling pin will suffice.
5. Heat a frying pan and add a little flour if necessary. Heat the Chapatti till bubbles or blisters appear. Cook on each side three to four minutes.

*   A nonstick pan is best to use. They can be baked on a cookie sheet or baking pan at 370oF. These could also be baked on a grill. Cracked wheat flour comes highly recommended.

# Paratha

This is the same recipe as Chappatti except 4 ounce of Ghee will be used, melted, and brushed on the dough before frying. Break the dough into 6 pieces. Roll each out on a floured board or table. They should be 3-4 inches in diameter. Brush on the ghee and roll them back into a ball. Then flatten them out at the most 5 inches. Heat and grease a pan with ghee or butter then fry each piece until they are golden brown.

—

# Puri

This is a deep fried "Balloon bread" and finally different from traditional breads. Since this is deep fried caution should be used as always.

1 cup of whole-wheat flour
1 cup of baking or all-purpose flour
1/2 cup of milk
pinch of sea salt
2 tbsp vegetable oil

1. Sift the flours into the same bowl and integrate them. Add salt and oil and mix in well.
2. Slowly add the milk and make the dough. Add extra flour if it seems too sticky.
3. Deposit this onto a working surface, add some flour so it does not stick and knead it till it is smooth and not sticky.
4. Set it aside for thirty minutes. Then roll it out again and divide them into twelve puris balls.
5. Heat a skillet or wok then add oil up to 1 inch. Oil should have a temperature of 370oF.
6. Place the Puri into the skillet and let it hit the bottom, it should rise up again, they should puff up. With a kitchen spoon pour a little oil over them and when they are golden brown, Remove them letting them drain on a paper towel.

# Roti

This is a simple bread as Chapatti is, and just as good.

2 cups Whole-wheat flour
1 cup white flour
1 cup of water (depending)
pinch of sea salt

1. Add the ingredients. in a bowl with little water at a time. The dough should be soft and pliable.
2. Knead this dough on a clean working surface spreading enough flour so it does not stick. It should be smooth and not sticky.
3. Let it sit for thirty minutes, then knead it again and break the dough into 8 to 10 balls.
4. Flatten these as Chappatti and either fry then in a pan, bake them at 470oF.
5. The traditional method is to place these on a grill and as one side bubbles and blisters, turn it over and cook them on the other side. Maybe 3-4 minutes each side.

*   These are often made in a tandoori oven, if you have such equipment then use a tandoori grill to cook them on.

# Chapatti

2 cups of white flour
1 tsp. baking powder
1 tsp. salt
1 tsp. sugar
1 tsp. dry active yeast
2/3 cup of milk
2/3 cup of plain yogurt
1 egg beaten

1.  sift the dry ingredients. in a bowl and integrate well.
2.  The milk and yogurt should be at room temperature. Add the dry active yeast. Mix well.
3.  Gradually mix in the yeast paste with the flour making a soft dough. On a clean surface add a little flour and knead the dough till it smooth and not sticky. Add the egg and knead again. Put the dough a side and let it rise two hours.
4.  Break the dough into eight pieces and flatten them out with the hand. Preheat oven at 4750oF and bake them till they are golden brown.

\*   As with many breads, you can put poppy, sesame, or any seed of choice upon them.

# Chicken

## Tandoori Chiken

1 Chicken
8 oz plain yogurt
1/2 cup lemon juice
1 tbsp curry powder
1 tsp. chili powder
1 tbsp ginger
1 tbsp cinnamon
4 cloves garlic (crushed)
1 yellow onion (sliced)
1 tbsp red food coloring
1 tbsp yellow food coloring

1. Except for the chicken add all the ingredients. in a mixer, blender, or food processor. It can be mixed by hand also it doesn't matter.
2. Place the chicken in a deep dish and marinate with the mix. Let it stand over night or 4 hours.
3. If you are barbecuing, place the chicken on hot grill and cook till done.
4. Or heat oven to 475o F and cook 45 minutes or till done.

* If you are using a indoor oven, use liquid smoke for authenticity.

# Chicken Korma

1 chicken (cut into pieces)
3/4 cup of unflavored yogurt
« cup of ghee
1 tbsp ginger powder
1 tsp.p cinnamon
1/4 cup coconut (shredded)
1/2 cup roasted almonds
1 tbsp curry powder
1 onion (sliced)
4 cloves garlic (crushed)

1.  Mix the spices into the yogurt and marinade the chicken over night or a few hours.
2.  Heat a skillet and add the ghee and spread it around the pan evenly. Add the onion and garlic and cook till fragrant.
3.  Place in the chicken and coconut in the skillet and cook till done. This should be simmered under a tight fitting lid maybe 45 minutes.

# Chicken Mougalai

1 chicken (cut in to pieces
4 tbsp ghee
1 cup of yogurt
1 tbsp black pepper
7 whole cardamom pods
8 whole cloves
1 tsp. cinnamon
1 tsp. cumin powder
1 tsp. red pepper flakes
2 bay leaves
1/4 to 1/2 cup of blanched almonds
1/2 cup blanched almonds
1/2 cup of golden raisin or sultanas

1. Sprinkle black pepper on the chicken. Heat oil and ghee in a skillet and place in the chicken, spices, bay leaves, cardamom pods, omitting the cumin and red pepper flakes. Cook chicken till browned on both sides.
2. In a bowl add the yogurt, cumin and pepper. Mix well. Add the almonds to the chicken and brown them. Then add the raisins.
3. A minute after adding the raisins add the yogurt and braise.
4. After chicken is cooked place it in a plate and pour any remaining sauce on top. The sauce should be a little thick. If not then reduce it in the pan for a short time.

# Chicken Biryani

1 cup of brown rice
2 cloves of garlic (crushed)
2 1/2 cups of chicken stock
1 red pepper (sliced)

—

1 cup white or basmati rice
2 tbsp butter
1 tsp. cinnamon
pinch of saffron or Kasuba
1 tsp. turmeric
1 bay leaf
2 tsp. ginger

—

1 chicken (cut into 1 or 2 inch pieces)
1 tbsp curry powder
1 tsp. turmeric powder
1 tsp. cumin powder
1 tsp. chili powder
1 tsp. black pepper
2 cups of yogurt
1/4 cup of golden raisins
2 onions ( cut into chunks)
1 onion (Sliced into rings)
4 cloves garlic (minced)
3 carrots (cut into cubes)
1/2 cup of cashews or peanuts. (or choice)
1/2 cup cilantro leaves

1. Cook the brown rice by boiling 2 cups of chicken broth and adding the brown rice ingredients.
2. Cook white or basmati rice using the separate ingredients. Only use 1 tsp. of ginger.
3. In a skillet brown the onion rings and set aside.
4. Sauté the Chicken browning both side. Except the raisins, cilantro, and nutsp.p, add the remaining ingredients. Do not cook the chicken all the way through.
5. Heat the oven to 475o F and in a 13 X 9 shallow baking dish add brown rice mix on one side, saffron mix on the other. Then pour the skillet contents on top distribute evenly. Add the raisins.
6. Cover top with foil Cook this 45 minutes or till done.

When it is out of the oven sprinkle onions and nutsp.p on top.

* This is the complex version of Bityani. You could go easier on yourself by cutting the recipe in half. You could also use either just the brown or saffron rice. Using smaller portions of the meat recipe is not a bad idea. You could use any meat with this. If you are using beef add beef broth to the brown rice. If you are going to use fish, don't cut it up, leave it whole. Fish will need less cooking time. Most of the recipes in this book will have the meat featured as the main ingredient. The meatsp.p are interchangeable, so use any meat you wish. This especially applies to Biryanis.

# Chicken Vindaloo

1 1/2 lb chicken (boned and cubed 3/4 inches)
2 onions (1 quartered, one sliced)
4 cloves garlic
1 tbs. ginger root or powder
1 tsp. black mustard seed (optional)
(or mustard powder)
1 tsp. cinnamon
1 tsp. ground cloves
1 tsp. cumin
1 1/2 tsp. turmeric
1 1/2 tsp. red pepper flakes
1 1/2 tsp. paprika
1 can tamarind juices
2 tbsp cider vinegar
2 tbsp light vegetable oil

1. Put onion, garlic, ginger, vegetable oil and cider vinegar in a blender and run the machine till it is a fine puree.
2. Take the chicken and put it in a glass bowl and marinade Adding cumin, and mustard, pureed mixture, and cinnamon and cloves. Let it marinate 6 to 8 hours. It is possible to refrigerate it for 48 hours.
3. Heat oil in a wok or skillet, add the sliced onions and cook till they are browned. Reduce heat if necessary and add the turmeric, red pepper, and paprika for ten seconds. Add the meat and marinade and stir fry till the meat is cooked. Add the tamarind juice and bring it to a boil. Serve this hot.

* If the tamarind juice is to bitter add a little brown or white sugar while you are cooking.

# Chicken Tari

1 1/2 lb chicken (boned and cubed 3/4 inch)
6 tbsp ghee or unsalted butter
1 onion (sliced)
1 tsp. cumin powder
2 tsp. coriander powder
1 tsp. turmeric
1 tsp. red pepper flakes
2 tbsp Coriander leaves
1/2 cup tomato puree

1. In a hot wok or skillet add ghee and melt it coating the vessel. Add the onions and caramelize. Then add the spices for 10 seconds. Finally add the pureed tomato and cook till it thickens a bit.
2. Add the chicken, with 2« cup of water, boil this till the chicken is done. This should have the consistency of vegetable soup.

*Make the sauce more flavorful by adding some ghee.

# Chicken Bhuna

1 1/2 lb chicken
1 cup of grated coconut
1/2 cup plain yogurt
2 green chilies
1 small onion (chopped)
2 tbsp Coriander leaves
1 tbsp black mustard seeds
2 tbsp ghee

1.  Place all the spices except the black mustard seed in a blender, accompanied by the yogurt and coconut. Run the machine to puree.
2.  Marinate the chicken with the puree for 8 hours.
3.  Heat a wok or skillet then add the ghee. Coat the pan and add the mustard seeds. When they turn gray, add the chicken. Cook till the chicken is done.

*   You will want to either cover or put a screen on top of the pan when roasting the mustard seeds. They tend to pop and sputter and it could make a slight mess. Adding a little curry powder to the puree will give it a spicier edge.

# Chicken Saagwala

1 1/2 lbs Chicken (boned and cubed 3/4 inch)
2 lbs spinach 0r 1 lb spinach with 1 lb of other greens
1 lb of potatoes (peeled and quartered)
2 cloves garlic (minced)
2 green chilies (minced)
1 tsp. cumin seeds
1 tsp. ginger powder
1 tsp. garam masala
5-6 tbsp ghee

1. Clean the greens and slice them thinly. If you are using frozen or canned green, defrost them and drain the water. Pat them with a paper towel if necessary.
2. Heat wok or skillet and add ghee, spread it around the pan and add cumin seeds. Fry then till they are dark, add the garlic and peppers.
3. Add chicken and potatoes and cook them till they are browned. Add the greens with 1¬ cup of water. Add the ginger powder and stir.
4. When the liquids almost are entirely evaporated and the greens are limp add the garam masala and stir integrating it well into the contents.

*   Always clean fresh greens. Discard any wilting, rotted, yellow leaves. Wash them in cold water and make sure any foreign matter is washed away.

*   There is a dish in which chicken tikka is used. When you do, this dish becomes Chicken tikka Saag. Other greens can be used like mustard, or kale.

# Chicken Makhani

1 tandoori chicken
3 cups tomato puree
4 Breen chilies (seeded)
4 slices ginger root (chopped)
1 1/4 stick sweet butter
1 1/2 cup heavy cream
4 tsp. cumin powder
1 tbsp paprika
2 tsp. gram masala
1/2 cup of coriander leaves

1. Cut the chicken in half and into pieces. Do not dice or De bone.
2. Make a puree of the tomato, ginger, and green chilies in a blender or food processor.
3. In a skillet melt 1 stick of butter and cook the chicken till the pieces are browned. If the pan seems small cook a bit of the chicken at a time and reserve in a bowl.
4. Add the cumin and paprika to the pan with the melted butter. Add the tomato puree and stir. Cook it 8 to ten minute.
5. Add the chicken and the cream to the skillet and stir fry. Coat the chicken with the sauce till it coats well and a thin glaze appears on the surface. Add the ¬ stick of butter and the garam masala and stir well. Blend in the coriander leaves. Mix it well and serve.

# Chicken Tikka Marsala

1 lb of chicken Tikka
2 onions (sliced)
1/4 stick of unsalted butter
1 1/2 cup tomato puree
2 tsp. garam masala

1. In a skillet or wok, melt the butter and coat the vessel evenly. Add the sliced onions and cook till browned.
2. Add the chicken tikka and stir it around in the pan for a few seconds. Than add the tomato puree.
3. When the tomato sauce simmers, add the garam masala and integrate well.

* We can make some variations on this dish by adding cilantro. Also the sauce could be embellished by adding either yogurt or coconut milk. Different spices such as turmeric, ginger, cumin, or your favorite would be expectable. A herb or two can be added such as bay leaf or curry leaf.

# Chicken Kasmir

1 1/2 lb of chicken (boned and cubed)
2 cups curry sauce
1/4 to « lb cashews
1/4 to « lb almonds (slivered)

1.  Make or use the traditional curry sauce. Brown the almonds in a skillet or wok. Remove and reserve.
2.  In a hot wok or skillet add oil and cook the chicken. Throw in the almonds and cashews and stir fry mixing frequently.
3.  When the chicken is almost done, add in the curry sauce and cook it till it is simmering and not boiling.

*  Alternatives to almonds and cashew can be used. Of course it would not be Chicken Kashmere anymore, but adding cardamom or peanuts. or any variety of your favorite nut is fine. Adding a yellow squash is fine also, just slice it and fry it till it is tender. remove it and reserve it and add it anytime to the cooking process. Don't make it mushy.

# LAMB

## Lamb Rogan Josh

3 lbs lamb (1« inch cubes)
4 onions (quartered)
4 cloves garlic (minced)
2 slices of ginger (julienne)
1/2 tsp. red pepper flakes
2 tbsp ground coriander
1 tbsp cumin
1 tsp. garam masala
2 tsp. cardamom powder
1/2 cup ghee
2 1/2 cups plain yogurt
1 cup cream
1/2 cup sour cream

1. Place onions, ginger, coriander, red pepper, yogurt, and sour cream Run the machine till it is well integrated, it must be smooth and not chunky.
2. In a bowl, add the lamb. Heat the ghee in a pan and when it is melted pour it over and coat the lamb. Then pour over the marinade. Let it stand 2 hours.
3. Heat a wok or skillet add the lamb and cook till it is done. It should be very tender.
4. In a small frying pan add the remaining ghee, coat the pan and add the garlic and spices. After 15 seconds add the cream an cook it till it is hot, but not boiling. Pour it over the lamb. Mix well.

# Seekh Kabobs

1 lb of ground lamb
2 tbsp garlic (crushed)
1 tsp. ginger (chopped)
1 1/2 tsp. cumin
1 tsp. coriander powder
1 tsp. paprika
1 tsp. garam masala
1 tsp. pepper
1 tsp. basil and/or mint
1 tsp. Kari leaves (crushed or powdered)
1/4 cup bread crumbs
1 tbsp sweet butter
1 egg (slightly beaten)

1. Put all the ingredients. in a bowl and mix thoroughly. Cover it and rest it for 2 hours. This kabob mixture should be used immediately afterward.
2. Remove kabob meat from the bowl and divide them up into 16 pieces. Take each and roll them into a sausage shape. Then place a skewer up the center of the sausage.
3. Heat the oven at 400oF. Place each kabob on a cooking sheet and bake for twenty minutes of till they are almost done. If you are not going to grill them let them cook thoroughly.
4. Place each on a grill above the coals and cook them through.

\* If you are using bamboo or wooden skewers soak them first so they do not splinter. Also is you are just going to oven cook them add a little liquid smoke. You could stuff these with almonds too.

# Keema Mutter

2 lbs ground lamb
2 onions (finely chopped)
2 cloves garlic (minced)
4 1 tsp. ginger powder
1 tsp. cumin
2 tsp. coriander
1 tsp. turmeric
1 tsp. red pepper flakes
2 bay leaves
2 cups of tomato (chopped)
3 tbsp cashew nut butter (optional)
1 can chick peas
2 tsp. garam masala
1 green chili (julienne)

1. Heat the oil in a wok or skillet and add the onions. Caramelize them. Be careful not to burn them. Add garlic and ginger and stir fry till fragrant or 15 seconds.
2. Add the spices and bay leaves mix them around in the pan. Then ad the lamb. Cook them till all traces of pink are gone. Add the chick peas, nut butter, and chopped tomatoes. Cook this until the sauce thickens.
3. During cooking, keep stirring so the meat does not stick or burn. When done turn off heat and add the garam masala and green chili pepper. Mix them thoroughly and serve at once.

* A substitution of nut butter by using ground cashews with sweet butter. Also, do not drain the chick pea cans of water. Use the water for cooking.

# Roti Kabob

1 lb lamb (1« inch cubes)
1/2 cup plain yogurt
1 onion (chopped)
3 cloves garlic (crushed)
1 tsp. turmeric
1 tsp. cumin
1 tsp. coriander powder
2 tsp. garam masala

1.  Place all the ingredients. in a bowl and marinade the lamb for 2 hours. Mix the ingredients. well.

2.  Using a metal skewer thread each piece of meat on it. Then place it in the oven at 475oF for 20 minutes or place in a grill and cook till the meat is thoroughly cooked.

* Normally this is done in a tandoori oven. A onion is placed at the end of the skewer so the meat doesn't slide off. The actual recipe calls for the use of curds rather then yogurt.

# VEGETABLES

## Aloo Beans

6 red potatoes
1 lb fresh green beans
1 small onion
2 tomatoes ( inch cubes)
1/4 cup coriander leaves
1/2 or 1/4 cup lemon juice
1 tsp. cumin
1/3 cup cold water
1 tsp. garam masala

1. Mix the masala in water and set it aside for a moment.
2. Boil the potatoes. You will not have to peel them since their skins are almost like paper. Drain them and peel them if you desire. Cut them into cubes at least « inch.
   Pour the masala mixture on them and integrate well. Let them sit at least 15 minutes till the water is absorbed. Stir a few times during the wait.
3. If you are using fresh green beans, clean them and boil them tie they are cooked. If you are using caned just heat them up. Drain them and add them to the potatoes after the 15 minutes are up.
4. Add the chopped onion tomato, and coriander leaves. Do not mix them.
5. Sprinkle cumin, and lemon juice over the Aloo and mix it well.

\* This dish may be served cold. Just refrigerate it and
then do step 5.

# Aloo Gobhi

6 red potatoes
1 lb fresh cauliflower
1 small onion
2 tomatoes (« inch cubes)
1/4 cup coriander leaves
1/2 cup lemon juice
1 tsp. cumin
1/3 cup cold water
1 tsp. garam masala

1.  Mix the masala in water and set it aside for a moment.
2.  Boil the potatoes. You will not have to peel them since their skins are almost like paper. Drain them and peel them if you desire. Cut them into cubes at least « inch.
    Pour the masala mixture on them and integrate well. Let them sit at least 15 minutes till the water is absorbed.
    Stir a few times during the wait.
3.  If you are using fresh Cauliflower, clean them and boil them till they are cooked. If you are using caned just heat them up. Drain them and add them to the potatoes after the 15 minutes are up.
4.  Add the chopped onion tomato, and coriander leaves. Do not mix them.
5.  Sprinkle cumin, and lemon juice over the Aloo gobhi and mix it well.

# Aloo Palak

6 red potatoes
1 lb fresh Spinach
1 small onion
2 tomatoes (« inch cubes)
1/4 cup coriander leaves
1/2 cup lemon juice
1 tsp. cumin
1/3 cup cold water
1 tsp. garam masala

1.  Mix the masala in water and set it aside for a moment.
2.  Boil the potatoes. You will not have to peel them since their skins
    are almost like paper. Drain them and peel them if you desire.
    Cut them into cubes at least « inch.
    Pour the masala mixture on them and integrate well. Let them
    sit at least 15 minutes till the water is absorbed.
    Stir a few times during the wait.
3.  If you are using fresh Spinach, clean them and boil them till
    they are cooked. If you are using caned just heat them up.
    Drain them and add them to the potatoes after the 15 minutes
    are up.
4.  Add the chopped onion tomato, and coriander leaves. Do not
    mix them.
5.  Sprinkle cumin, and lemon juice over the Aloo gobhi and mix
    it well.

# Bartha

2 egg plants (1 lb each)
« cup of peas
1 small onion (chopped)
1 tsp. garlic (minced)
3 slices ginger root (julienne)
1/3 cup vegetable oil
2 tomatoes (chopped)
2 green chilies (sliced and seeded)
1/4 cup coriander leaves

1.  Take the egg plants wash them. Heat the oven on broil.
    Dry off the egg plants and put them on a broiling rack and cook
    them. Turn them over frequently. They are cooked when their
    skins are slightly chard and very soft.
    Remove them and peel the skin off.
2.  When the skin is removed, make the egg plant into a puree.
    It should be so soft that there will be no problem in doing
    So, This can be done in a bowl or food processor.
3.  Cook the peas in hot water till they are done. If they are fresh
    make sure they are shelled. If frozen, follow the package
    directions.
4.  Heat a wok or skillet and add some oil. Fry some garlic and
    ginger for 15 seconds then add onions and cook them till they
    are alight golden color. Stir to prevent scorching and do not
    caramelize them.
5.  Add the tomatoes and chili peppers, with the puree. Cook them
    till the tomatoes break down to softness. Add the peas and cook
    till the peas are hot. Remove them from the heat and add the
    coriander leaves.

# Bhindi Masala

1 lb of Okra
2 onions (sliced)
1/4 stick of unsalted butter
1 1/2 cup tomato puree
2 tsp. garam masala

1.  In a skillet or wok, melt the butter and coat the vessel evenly. Add the sliced onions and cook till browned.
2.  Add the Okra and stir it around in the pan for a few seconds. Than add the tomato puree.
3.  When the tomato sauce simmers, add the garam masala and integrate well. It is finished cooking when the okra is soft and tender

* With okra it is important to remove stems. If the okra is very large it is okay to slice it. Panir and/or Chick peas may substitute the okra

# Dal Tarka

1 1/2 cups yellow split peas
1 onion (chopped)
4 cloves garlic (chopped)
4 slices of ginger (julienne)
1 tsp. mustard or black mustard seeds
1 tsp. turmeric
1 tsp. cumin
1 tsp. red pepper powder
1/2 cup of ghee
1/4 cup coriander leaves

1.  Wash the peas and soak them in hot water, covering them by 1 inch for 1 hour.
2.  Put the peas in a large pot and add the turmeric. Add 4« cups of water. Bring this to a boil and cook the peas for 45 minutes or till they are soft. They should be somewhat mushy. Then remove them from the heat and puree them using a wire whisk.
3.  Heat a wok or skillet and « cup of ghee. stir it around the pan
4.  Add the onion, garlic, pepper, ginger, and spices. Cook them till the onions are golden brown. Then pour this over the puree. Top it with the coriander and serve.

* There is a spice available in India grocery stores called asafetida. This can be added to most dishes. It is a condiment made of different resins and brown in color. It may keep for many years.

# Palak Panir

1 cup spinach (fresh or canned)
1 cup panir
1 tsp. cumin
1 tsp. coriander
1 tsp. black and red pepper
1 tsp. paprika

1. Coarsely chop spinach with a knife or use a food processor.
2. Cut the panir into cubes and put them in a bowl with spinach.
3. Then add the spices and integrate thoroughly.

\* One could make a Raita out of this by adding 1« cup of yogurt and 1 cup of sour cream. Adding a sliced cucumber and mint would be a plus.

# Mushroom Sag

1 1/2 lbs mushrooms
2 lbs spinach 0r 1 lb spinach with 1 lb of other greens
1 lb of potatoes (peeled and quartered
2 cloves garlic (minced)
2 green chilies (minced)
1 tsp. cumin seeds
1 tsp. ginger powder
1 tsp. garam masala
5-6 tbsp ghee

1. Clean the greens and slice them thinly. If you are using frozen or canned green, defrost them and drain the water. Pat them with a paper towel if necessary.
2. Heat wok or skillet and add ghee, spread it around the pan and add cumin seeds. Fry then till they are dark, add the garlic and peppers.
3. Add mushrooms and potatoes and cook them till the potatoes brown. Add the greens with 1 1/4 cup of water. Add the ginger powder and stir.
4. When the liquids almost are entirely evaporated and the greens are limp add the garam masala and stir integrating it well into the contents. Serve in individual bowls.

# THAILAND

Sauces: These sauces and condiments are essential in Thailand's cuisine, here are the basics that are necessary.

## Satay Peanut Sauce

1 can of coconut milk
1 cup of water
1 cup of crunchy peanut butter(smooth if desired)
2 tbsp sesame oil
juice of 1 or 2 limes
1 tbsp shrimp paste
4 cloves garlic (crushed)
2 red hot chili peppers (chopped)
pinch salt (only if absent from peanut butter)
2 tbsp honey ( a dark variety)

1.  In a skillet heat oil and fry garlic a few seconds.
2.  Add all the rest of the ingredients. and stir well. Cook for 7 to 8 minutes or more.

*   This is a all purpose condiment used in all kinds of cooking. Shrimp paste in Thai is called Kapi just in case you are near a China town and working with imported items.

# Padang Sauce

1/2cup peanut butter (smooth or chunky)
or 10 to i5 roasted peanuts. (grounded)
1 tbsp peanut oil
4 cloves garlic (crushed)
1 tbsp Chili powder or Chili paste
1 tbsp tamarind juice
1 tbsp brown sugar
1 1/4 cup water
1 tbsp fish sauce
1/2 cup soybean sauce (Not soy sauce but tuong) optional

1.  Heat wok or skillet and fry the garlic till browned.
2.  Make a paste out of peanut butter, chili powder, tamarind juice, sugar, fish sauce, garlic, and tuong.
3.  This should be made in a food processor or blender. Using manual method is ok.
4.  Bring the water to a boil and add paste. Lower heat a bit and stir the sauce till it loosely thickens.

# Sweet and Sour Sauce

1 cup water
1/2 cup rice vinegar
2 tbsp tomato paste or ketchup
Pinch of salt
1 tsp. red pepper flakes
1/2 cup of sugar
2 tbsp corn starch dissolved in 4 tbsp water

1. Bring the water to a boil and add all the ingredients., except
   gradually add the cornstarch. Stir till it is loosely thick.

*  For S&S peanut sauce eliminate ketchup or tomato paste and
add satay

# Nam Prik Gang Massman Curry Paste

10 dried chilies
8 cloves of garlic
1 large onion chopped
4 tbsp fine chopped lemon grass or
1 tsp. Citron powder or oil
1 tsp. galangal (powdered)
4 bay leaves
2 tsp. coriander (greens or ground seeds)
1 tsp. cumin
1 tsp. nutmeg
1 tsp. cardamom powder (or 5 pods)
1 tsp. ginger
1 tsp. blank pepper

—

## Green Curry Paste/Red Curry Paste/Yellow Curry Paste

10 green chilies (chopped)
or 10 red chilies (chopped) used for yellow curry
6 cloves garlic
1 onion(chopped)
1 tsp. galangal
1 tsp. lemon grass
1/2 cup coriander (greens)
2 tsp. ground coriander ( For Yellow Curry add Turmeric instead)
1 tsp. cumin
1 tsp. Shrimp paste
Pinch of sea salt

Put these all in a food processor or blender and turn them into paste. These will be cooked dry or with coconut milk.

# APPETIZERS

## Satay

1 lb meat of choice (cubed)
1 tbsp Curry powder
satay sauce

1. Place meat in a bowl and sprinkle on curry powder. Then add the satay sauce. Marinate for several hours.
2. Thread each piece on a bamboo skewer and put them in a safe place.
3. On a grill or in a oven cook them 475oF twenty minutes or more.

—

# Tod Mun Pla-Thai fish Cake

1 lb of flounder or fish of choice
1 tbsp fish sauce
1 egg white
1/4 cup red curry paste
2 kaffir lime leaves (chopped fine)
salt if necessary

1. Mince the flounder finely. Then mix all the other ingredients.
   into the fish.
2. Make a, if possible, 2 inch patty out of the mix.
3. Heat a skillet and add enough oil, not too much, 1 inch and fry
   the patties till they are golden brown.

* If you want them hotter add red pepper flakes. Put a
little oil in your hands if the fish is too sticky.

# Deep Fried Tofu With Sweet And Sour Sauce

1 cake tofu
Sweat and Sour Peanut Sauce
1 egg (beaten)
1 cup rice flour

1.  Cut the tofu in 1« by 1 inch cubes. Dip them in eggs then rice flour.
2.  Heat two cups of oil in Wok or skillet 370oF and dip each coated tofu piece in them. Cook them till they are golden brown.
3.  Divide them and place sweet and sour sauce in small plates and dip them as you eat them.
4.  Or coat them in hot sweet and sour peanut sauce.

\* One could make a coating by browning to a gold color short grain rice in a frying pan or wok. Do not burn it. Then grind it down to a powder. You could probably by this in a Thai or South East Asian supermarket. One could even brown the rice flour in a pan. If you are feeling ambitious you could make a slit « inch in the middle and add baby shrimp. A little fried coconut and almond grounded down would be a interesting treat.

# Thai Salad

1 small head lettuce (shredded)
1/4 to 1 cucumber (julienne)
1 tomato (sliced)
4 cloves garlic (crushed)
1 small head romaine lettuce
1 onion (sliced)
5 scallions (sliced)
1 potato (thinly sliced as chips and fries)
1 cup padang sauce
1/2 cup roasted peanuts.(broken up)

1. Peel potato and slice it paper thin. He a skillet or wok and add 1 inch of oil. Fry the pieces till brown. Let them cool while draining on a paper towel.
2. Add all the ingredients. in a bowl and except satay and peanuts. and potato chips.
3. Divide each in a serving bowl, add the peanuts., then chips, then Padang sauce.

\* If the Padang sauce is to thick, loosen it up with a little oil and water evenly.

# Yum Nurr-Thai Beef Salad

1 lb beef
4 cloves garlic
1 small head romaine lettuce
1 onion (sliced)
1 cucumber (halved and sliced)
1 tomato (sliced)
2 red chilies (sliced)
2 scallions (sliced)
1 tbsp. fish sauce
2 tbsp. lime juice
1 tsp. sugar
1 tsp. black or white pepper
1/4 cup coriander
1/4 cup mint leaves
5 tbsp. toasted rice (optional)

1. Broil beef in oven on broiler pan, or cook it over coals. It is tastier when one uses wood chips like hickory.
2. When beef is cooked slice it thin. Then in a bowl after the beef has cooled add the vegetables and beef and toss it.

* Wood chips can be found at the out door grill section of a department store.

# Yum Woon Sen-Vermicelli And Shrimp Salad

1 lb shrimp (shelled and de-veined
1 small head romaine lettuce (Shredded)
1 inch piece of ginger (Julienne)
8 oz rice vermicelli noodles
4 cloves garlic (crushed)
1 onion (sliced)
1 stalk lemon grass (crushed)
2 red chilies (sliced)
2 scallions (sliced)
1 tbsp fish sauce
2 tbsp lime juice
1 tsp. sugar
1 tsp. black or white pepper
1/4 cup coriander
1/4 cup mint leaves
2 scallions (Chopped)

1. Bring pot of water to a boil, and the shrimp and cook for 2 minutes or till pink.
2. In another pot if desired, boil water and cook vermicelli to package directions. Drain in colander.
3. Mix all in a bowl and top with the Scallions, mint leaves, and coriander. Yes, you may feel free to mix them in.

# SOUPS

## Tom Kha Gai-Chicken In Coconut Broth

1 lb chicken breast (sliced or shredded)
2 tsp. lime juice
1/4 cup fish sauce
1 can coconut milk
3 cups chicken broth
1 tsp. red curry paste
1 stalk lemon grass (chopped)
2 green chilies (chopped)
5 kaffir lime leaves (chopped)
1 tsp. galangal
2 tbsp corn starch
5 to 10 shiitake mushrooms
2 tbsp oil

1.  Heat work or kettle and add oil, stir fry all dry ingredients. including red curry paste and green chilies. 1 or 2 minutes.
2.  Add chicken broth and bring it to a boil.
3.  Dip the chicken in corn starch and add it to the broth.
4.  Add coconut milk, mushrooms, fish sauce, and lime juice. Simmer till chicken is completely white and cooked through.

# Tom Yum Goong Shrimp In Clear Broth

1 lb shrimp (shelled and de-veined
6 cups of water
2 tbsp lime juice
1/4 cup fish sauce
4 chilies 2 red,2 green(chopped)
1 stalk lemon grass (chopped)
1 purple or red onion(chopped)
5 kaffir lime leaves (chopped)
1 tsp. galangal
6 cloves garlic (crushed)
4 tbsp coriander or « cup of chopped coriander
2 tbsp oil

1. Heat oil in wok or skillet and stir fry garlic and onions till they are browned.
2. Add the water and bring it to a boil. Add all the dry ingredients. including chilies. boil for 2 minutes.
3. Add the remaining ingredients. except for coriander. Boil the shrimp till they are pink. Then add the coriander and serve

# Tom Yum Gai-Chicken In A Clear Broth

1 lb chicken breast (sliced)
6 cups of water
2 tbsp lime juice
1/4 cup fish sauce
4 chilies 2 red,2 green(chopped)
1 stalk lemon grass (chopped)
1 purple or red onion(chopped)
5 kaffir lime leaves (chopped)
1 tsp. galangal
6 cloves garlic (crushed)
4 tbsp coriander or « cup of chopped coriander
2 tbsp oil

1. Heat oil in wok or skillet and stir fry garlic and onions till they
   are browned.
2. Add the water and bring it to a boil. Add all the dry ingredients.
   including chilies. boil for 2 minutes.
3. Add the remaining ingredients. except for coriander. Boil the
   chicken till it is white. Then add the coriander and serve.

# Kang Chud

1 lb chicken breast (sliced)
6 cups chicken stock
1 tsp. white pepper
1 tbsp preserved cabbage
5 cloves of garlic (crushed)
1 tbsp fish sauce
6 shiitake mushrooms
5 scallions (sliced)
1/4 cup coriander
4 oz tofu (cubed)
1 can bamboo shoots. (sliced)
1 green sweet or hot pepper (sliced)
8 oz rice vermicelli

1. In a pot bring the stock to a boil. Add the chicken, vegetables, herbs, and spices. Simmer till the chicken is almost cooked.
2. Add the vermicelli and cook for 2 to 3 minutes or till tender.
3. Distribute evenly in bowls.

# VEGETABLES

## Sauteed Eggplant

3 long green eggplants of choice
5 to 10 sprigs of Basil (whole or chopped)
10 cloves of garlic (crushed)
20 red chilies (chopped)
2 tbsp fish sauce
1/4 cup lime juice
2 tbsp brown sugar

1.  Slice off end of egg plants, and if desired peel off skin. Halve and thinly slice egg plants.
2.  Make a paste of the paste of the remaining ingredients., sans basil, in a blender or food processor. Place in a seal able container when done. It should be a smooth paste.
3.  Heat wok or skillet, add a the old and stir fry the eggplants. Add the sweet basil. When the eggplant is almost done add 4 to 7 tsps of the chili sauce. Stir fry till it is completely cooked. Not to soft or mushy, avoid this. El Dente!

\* One could easily buy this hot chili sauce at the Chinese or Thai Grocery stores. You may have to add lime juice and fish sauce. Tofu fans will love this sauce on there menu.

# Broccoli In Oyster Sauce

1 or 2 packages of frozen broccoli
2 tbsp oyster sauce
1 tbsp rice wine
2 tbsp corn starch dissolved in 4 tbsp water
1 tbsp soy sauce
2 tsp. sesame oil

1.  Thaw out or microwave frozen broccoli. Do not over cook.
2.  Heat a wok or skillet and then add the oil. Add the broccoli and stir fry till they are soft but not mushy.
3.  In a little custard bowl mix the wet ingredients. This should be done before or during Stir frying the broccoli.
4.  Pour in the oyster sauce preparation and coat he broccoli, add the cornstarch mixture and thicken up the juices.

*   This is a basic oyster sauce on could use on anything.

# String Beans In Garlic Sauce

14 oz of string beans
7 to 10 cloves of garlic (crushed)
2 tbsp of Chili oil or
4 tbsp of chili paste

1.  Remove stems and ends from string beans. These should be scalded in boiling water till they are soft, yet still have a firmness.
2.  In a small heated frying pan add oil, then the garlic and fry till fragrant. Add the soy sauce and chili oil or paste. Stir till everything integrates. This should take two minutes.
3.  Heat wok or skillet and then add the oil. Add the string beans and fry till they are done. Add the Garlic sauce and coat everything well.

# Sauteed Mixed Vegitables

1 Cake of bean curd (diced)
1 can of bamboo shoots. (sliced)
4 or 5 Shiitake mushrooms (sliced)
1 cab of Baby corn
1 onion (sliced)
1 green or red sweet pepper (sliced thinly)
2 or 3 scallions (sliced)
2 cloves garlic (crushed)
2 tbsp lime juice
1 tsp. white pepper
1 tbsp fish sauce
1 tbsp soy sauce
1 tbsp red pepper flakes

1.  Heat wok or skillet and add oil. Heat up the vegetables till they are hot, onions should be translucent.
2.  Add the rest of the ingredients. and integrate well while stir frying.

*   Adding a little cellophane noodles to this is a good idea. This could be a curry dish by adding red curry when frying, 2 tbsp chili paste, and sweet basil.

# Thai Fried Rice

4 cups of Jasmine rice or sticky rice
2 eggs (beaten)
1 yellow onion (chopped)
2 scallions chopped
1/4cup of coriander
1 1/2 to 2 lbs of meat or combinations
2 cloves of garlic
2 tbsp fish sauce
2 hot chili peppers (julienne)
1 tsp. white or black pepper

1.  Cook the rice by boiling 8 cups of water, when the water is absorbed the rice is cooked. Cover and set aside and allow it to steam 1 hour.
2.  In a skillet, add oil and cook the eggs. Scramble them first then allow them to cook.
3.  Heat wok or skillet, add oil. Fry the garlic till fragrant. Add the meat, fish sauce, chilies, and peppers. Stir fry till cooked.
4.  Add the rice and eggs. Stir fry for 2 minutes integrating everything. When done garnish with scallions and coriander.

*   Cook each meat separately, then add the condiments during the final process, before adding the rice and egg.

# Pad Thai-Thai Fried Noodles

1 lb chicken (sliced)
12 oz thin rice noodles
4 oz tofu (diced)
1 small Daikon (Asian radish) (Julienne)
2-4 scallions (sliced)
4 clove garlic (crushed
1 onion (sliced)
2 tbsp lime juice
2 tbsp fish sauce
2 fresh hot chili peppers
3 tbsp tamarind juice
1 tbsp sugar
8 oz bean sprouts.
1 tbsp coriander
1/2 cup roasted peanuts. (chopped)

1. Cook pasta according to package directions. As with all pastas keep stirring them so they do not stick. When done drain them in a colander.
2. Heat wok or skillet and add the oil, stir fry the garlic and onions till browned. Add the chicken and chilies.
3. Add the rest of the ingredients. sans coriander, peanuts., and scallions. Reserve Rice pasta till the very end.
4. When chicken is pink add the pasta and integrate for 1 minute.
5. Transfer to a serving platters and top with peanuts., coriander, and scallions.

* Thai Spaghetti: 8 oz of wide rice pasta of choice

1 cup of Padang Sauce. Top with coriander greens.

# Mee Krob-Crispy Pasta

1lb Shrimp
1lb pork loin (julienne)
1 chicken breast (boned and shredded)
8 oz rice vermicelli noodles
4 oz Tofu (cubed 1 by ( inches)
1/2 cup of bean sprouts.
4 cloves garlic
6 large shiitake mushrooms
1/4 cup fresh coriander
2 red chilies cut into strips
2 tbsp lime juice
2 tbsp soy sauce (light preferred but optional)
4 tbsp fish sauce.
1 tsp. sugar
2 cups of oil

* This is a two wok meal.

1. In a hot wok or skillet add two tbsp. of oil and cook the garlic till fragrant.
2. Add the meats and cook for 5 minutes, then add the rest of the ingredients. sans vermicelli.
3. In another wok or skillet heat oil to 370oF or test by dropping on piece of vermicelli. When it bubbles and cooks add the rest of the vermicelli.

* Add it dry! Do not soak it in water!

It will puff up immediately then turn it on the other side a few seconds. Remove and drain on a paper towel.

4. In separate plates add the vermicelli and meat mixture un top

# DUCK

## Keang Ped Ped Yang-Red Curry Duck

1 roasted duck (cut into pieces)
1 can coconut milk
« cup red curry paste
4 cloves garlic (crushed)
2 kaffir lime leaves (sliced)
1 tsp. ground coriander
1 tbsp red pepper flakes
2 tbsp lime juice
1 tsp. white or black pepper

1. Marinate duck with ground coriander, red pepper flakes, lime juice, white or black pepper for 20 minutes.
2. Preheat broiler and place duck on broiler pan, insert in oven and cook for 45 minutes or till meat is thoroughly cooked leaving the bone. When done slice it up.
3. Or as above one may roast it over coals.
4. Heat a wok or skillet and add oil then fry garlic briefly. Add the duck and curry paste. Stir fry for one minute, then add the coconut milk and bring it to a boil add the Kaffir lime leaves and cook for 2 minutes.

# Duck Pad Pring-Duck And Chili Sauce

1 roasted duck (cut into pieces)
4 cloves garlic (crushed)
2 kaffir lime leaves (sliced)
1 tsp. ground coriander
1 tbsp red pepper flakes
2 tbsp lime juice
1 tsp. white or black pepper
4 tbsp of chili paste

1. Marinate duck with ground coriander, red pepper flakes, lime juice, white or black pepper for 20 minutes.
2. Preheat broiler and place duck on broiler pan, insert in oven and cook for 45 minutes or till meat is thoroughly cooked leaving the bone. When done slice it up.
3. Or as above one may roast it over coals.
4. Heat wok or skillet add a little oil and fry garlic till fragrant. Then add the duck and fry till it is covered with chili sauce.

# Duck With Mixed Vegetables

1 roasted duck (cut into pieces)
4 cloves garlic (crushed)
1 small can baby corn
4 scallions
2 tbsp lime juice
1 tsp. white pepper
1 tbsp fish sauce
1 tbsp soy sauce
1 tbsp red pepper flakes
4 tbsp Kaffir lime leaves
8 Shiitake mushrooms (sliced)

1. Marinate duck with ground coriander, red pepper flakes, lime juice, white or black pepper for 20 minutes.
2. Preheat broiler and place duck on broiler pan, insert in oven and cook for 45 minutes or till meat is thoroughly cooked leaving the bone. When done slice it up.
3. Or as above one may roast it over coals.
4. Heat wok or skillet and add oil. Fry Garlic till fragrant.
5. Add fish and soy sauces. Add Shiitake mushrooms, baby corn, and scallions, and Kaffir lime leaves. Stir fry till the are hot. Then Stir Fry the duck 3 minutes.

# Thai Chicken

1 roasted chicken (cut into pieces)
4 cloves garlic (crushed)
1 small can baby corn
4 scallions
2 tbsp lime juice
1 tsp. white pepper
1 tbsp fish sauce
1 tbsp soy sauce
1 tbsp red pepper flakes
4 tbsp Kaffir lime leaves
8 Shiitake mushrooms (sliced)

1. Marinate Chicken with ground coriander, red pepper flakes, lime juice, white or black pepper for 20 minutes.
2. Preheat broiler and place chicken on broiler pan, insert in oven and cook for 45 minutes or till meat is thoroughly cooked leaving the bone. When done slice it up.
3. Or as above one may roast it over coals.
4. Heat wok or skillet and add oil. Fry Garlic till fragrant. Add fish and soy sauces. Add Shiitake mushrooms, baby corn, and scallions, and Kaffir lime leaves. Stir fry till the are hot. Then Stir Fry the chicken 3 minutes.

# Keang Kari Gai-Yellow Curry Chicken

1 op 2 chicken breasts (cooked and sliced)
1 can bamboo shoots. sliced
4 sprigs of sweet basil (sliced or crushed)
2 red Chilies (sliced)
1/4 cup coriander greens
Green Curry paste
1 or two cans coconut milk

1. Heat wok or skillet and add oil. Cook the bamboo shoots., and red chilies till hot. Add the curry and stir it around the mix in the chicken breast and stir fry a few minutes.
2. Add the Coconut milk and bring it to a boil. Cook 1 to 2 minutes. Top with coriander greens.

* The chicken breast can be made as previous recipe or plain. One could add squash or mangos instead of bamboo shoots. When increasing recipe add to proportion or when doubling double the rest of the ingredients. One could add coriander greens while cooking. Yellow curry is good for chicken. Adding tomatoes instead of a bamboo shoot is recommended. Add four tomatoes and quartered.

# Gai Young-Grilled Chicken

1/2 chicken
8 cloves garlic (crushed)
4 Kaffir lime leaves (sliced)
1/2 cup coriander leaves
1 tbs. red pepper flakes
5 to 10 sweet basil leaves (crushed)
2 tbsp lime juice
Serve with sweet and sour sauce in individual bowls.

1.  Put the chicken in a bowl. Place the condiments in another bowl and mix them together and coat the chicken with them for 20 minutes or overnight.
2.  Heat up coals in pit and place chicken on a grill and cook over the coals. Grilling should 45 minutes or till meat leaves the bone and it is all white.
3.  This can be done on the broiler grill in a oven. You may want to add liquid smoke.

*   There are stove top grills, mostly available in Korean stores. Theses are excellent and safe to use. Be cautious with other devices read the safety labels.

# Kai Phad King-Chicken With Ginger

1 Chicken breast (Cooked and Sliced)
1 to 1 1/2 inch ginger (Julienne/thinly)
4 cloves garlic (crushed)
4 scallions (sliced)
2 rice wine
1 tsp. white pepper
1/2 to small onion (sliced)
1 tbsp soy sauce (Tuong if available)
1 tbsp red pepper flakes
8 Shiitake mushrooms (sliced)

1. Heat oil in wok or skillet cook garlic till fragrant, then add the chicken and stir fry that 2 minutes. Then add shiitake mushrooms and fry another minute.
2. Add the rest of the ingredients. and cook till the chicken is done.

* Many varieties of mushrooms are now available. You may wish to try tree ears. Traditional mushrooms are also good. There are many excellent local varieties. Avoid those ugly slippery ones.

# Pad Gai Mauamg Himapan-Chicken With Cashews

1lb Chicken breast (Cooked and Sliced)
4 cloves garlic
1 slice of ginger
2 red chilies (sliced)2 tbsp lime juice
2 tbsp soy sauce (light preferred but optional)
2 tbsp Oyster Sauce
1 tsp. Soy Sauce (Tuong)
1 tsp. sugar
1 cup roasted cashew nuts
1/4 cup fresh coriander
1/4 cup corn starch

1. Heat wok or skillet then add oil. While pan is heating coat the chicken with corn starch. Add Garlic and ginger and fry till fragrant. put in the chicken and stir fry till browned.
2. Add liquid ingredients. and stir fry till slightly thickened.
3. Then add the remaining ingredients. and stir fry 2 to 3 minutes.

* You can top this with toasted sesame seeds.

# BEEF

## Exotic Thai Barbeque Beef

1/2 lb beef
8 cloves garlic (crushed)
4 Kaffir lime leaves (sliced)
1/2 cup coriander leaves
1 tbsp red pepper flakes
5 to 10 sweet basil leaves (crushed)
2 tbsp soy sauce
2 tbsp fish sauce
Serve with chilie sauce in individual bowls.

1. Put the beef in a bowl. Place the condiments in another bowl and mix them together and coat the beef with them for 20 minutes or overnight.
2. Heat up coals in pit and place beef on a grill and cook over the coals. Grilling should 45 minutes or till meat leaves the bone and it is all white. Slice the beef thinly.
3. This can be done on the broiler grill in a oven. You may want to add liquid smoke.

*   Serve this on a bed of rice noodles, or lettuce with cucumbers slices around the plate.

# Beef Masamam

1. Lb of beef (sliced thin)
Masaman curry paste
2 tbs. chili paste
Marinade from the previous recipe
1 or 2 cans coconut milk

1.  Put the beef in a bowl. Place the condiments in another bowl and mix them together and coat the beef with them for 20 minutes or overnight.
2.  In a wok or skillet heat the chili paste and curry 1 minute. Add the beef and stir fry till cooked.
3.  Add the coconut milk and bring to a boil.

\* This is muslam curry it is a tradition to cook this dish with beef or chicken, but never pork. This dish is from India originally. It reminds me of Korma just a little bit.

# Satay Beef

1 lb of beef chunks
red curry paste (liberal)
Satay sauce (Liberal)

1. Marinade the beef chunks using barbecue marinade ingredients.
2. Then add curry paste and satay sauce and spread it all around.
3. Let it stand two hours or over night.
4. Heat the coals in a grill or heat the oven 475o F. String beef on bamboo or metal skewers ( it doesn't matter) and place them on the grill or oven. Cook for 20 to 40 minutes or till meat is cooked.

* To garnish lay it on a bed of lettuce and cucumbers with or with out sliced tomatoes.

# Paneang Nuea

1 lb beef (sirloin preferred, cut into 1 inch cubes)
2 cans of coconut milk
1 tsp. coriander (ground)
1 tsp. white pepper
1 tbsp brown sugar
10 to 12 sweet basil leaves
2 Kaffir lime leaves (sliced)
1 tsp. Galangal
1 stalk lemon grass (chopped in 1 inch pieces)
2 tbsp peanut butter of choice
2-4 tbsp roasted peanuts. (crushed)
1/4 to 1/2 coriander leaves (chopped)
2 tbsp chili paste

1. Heat wok or soup pan and add oil when hot. Add the chili paste and beef and stir fry till brown.
2. Add the coconut milk and all the other ingredients. and bring it to a boil.
3. Reduce heat and simmer till the coconut milk has thickened. This is done when meat is completely cooked through.

# Beef and Broccoli in Oyster Sauce

1lb beef (cook as previous pages and sliced)
1 or 2 packages of frozen broccoli
2 tbsp oyster sauce
1 tbsp rice wine
2 tbsp corn starch dissolved in 4 tbsp water
1 tbsp soy sauce
2 tsp. sesame oil

1. Thaw out or microwave frozen broccoli. Do not over cook.
2. Heat wok or skillet and cook beef till browned.
3. Add the broccoli and stir fry till they are soft but not mushy.
4. In a little custard bowl mix the wet ingredients. This should be done before or during the stir frying of the beef and broccoli.
5. Pour in the oyster sauce preparation and coat the beef and broccoli cornstarch mixture and thicken up the juices.

# Garlic Chili Beef

1 lb beef (sliced)
5 to 10 sprigs of Basil (whole or chopped)
10 cloves of garlic (crushed)
20 red chilies (chopped)
2 tbsp fish sauce
1/4 cup lime juice
2 tbsp brown sugar

1.  Marinade the beef as in the Barbecue recipe.
2.  Make a paste of the remaining ingredients., sans basil, in a blender or food processor. Place in a seal able container when done. It should be a smooth paste.
3.  Heat wok or skillet, add a the old and stir fry the beef till browned. Add the sweet basil. When the beef is almost done add 4 to 7 tsp. of the chili Paste. Stir fry till it is completely cooked.

*   The chili paste recipe above can be used and goes recommended. In Chinese stores get it with extra garlic. Feel free to experiment with different methods of preparation in this book. I free lance all the time.

# SEA FOOD

## Shrimp in Yellow Curry

2 lbs medium chicken
4 small potatoes (sliced)
1 or 2 tbsp yellow curry paste
1 can coconut milk
3 cloves garlic(crushed)
1 tbsp lime juice
1 tsp. white or black pepper
1 red chili pepper (sliced)
2 tsp. sweet basil or lemon basil (chopped)

1. Heat wok or skillet, add oil, stir fry the potatoes till they are browned.
2. Add the rest of the ingredients., except the coconut milk. Fry till the chicken are pink, then add the coconut milk and heat it ill hot. Add Basil last.

*   Make sure you cook the potatoes so they are not falling apart. It is ok to use canned potatoes. You could add more curry paste as you prefer. Other curries as red and green can be used.

# Stir Fry Shrimp

2 lbs shrimp
1 small can baby corn
4 scallions
2 cloves garlic (crushed)
2 tbsp lime juice
1 tsp. white pepper
1 tbsp fish sauce
1 tbsp soy sauce
1 tbsp red pepper flakes

1. Heat wok or skillet, add oil then garlic. Cook till fragrant.
2. Add scallions shrimp and all the other ingredients. to and cook till the shrimp is cooked.

*   As you can see this is very basic. You can keep adding to this as many condiments as you like, such as basil, sweet or lemon. Lemon grass, Kaffir lime leaves. Coriander or mint of all varieties. Even spearmint. If the lime is too tart, cut it with a tsp. of sugar, as one would with tamarind.

# Shrimp with Garlic and Peppers

2 lbs shrimp
10 cloves garlic (crushed)
2 green or red sweet peppers (julienne)
2 tbsp lime juice
1 tsp. white pepper
1 tbsp fish sauce
1 tbsp soy sauce
1 tbsp red pepper flakes

1. Heat wok or skillet, add oil, and stir fry peppers till they are slightly soft. Remove from pan.
2. Add the garlic and cook till fragrant. add the rest of the ingredients. and return the pepper to the wok. Stir fry till shrimp turns pink.

\* A bed of rice pasta or vermicelli is recommended. Cook them to package directions. If you really want to go authentic with most meals serve a side if Jasmine rice and with Thailand tea-hot or iced.

# Satay Shrimp

1 lb of shrimp
yellow curry paste (liberal)
satay sauce (Liberal)

1.  Marinade the shrimp using barbecue marinade ingredients.
2.  Then add curry paste and satay sauce and spread it all around.
3.  Let it stand two hours or over night.
4.  Heat the coals in a grill or heat the oven 475o F. String shrimp on bamboo or metal skewers ( it doesn't matter) and place them on the grill or oven. Cook for 3 to 4 minutes or till Shrimp turns pinkish.

\*   To garnish lay it on a bed of lettuce and cucumbers with or with out sliced tomatoes.

# Khao Pad Prik

1 lb shrimp
3 cups cooked rice
1/4 cup coriander leaves
2 scallions (sliced)
1 yellow onion (chopped)
4 cloves garlic (crushed)
1 carrot (peeled and chopped)
8 oz green beans (chopped)
1 can bamboo shoots. (sliced)
1 8 oz can pineapple chunks
red curry paste

1. Steam the shrimp in a steamer till pink. Cook the rice, 3 cups to 6 cups of water, till all the water is absorbed. Keep a lid on the pot of rice for 15 to 30 minutes.
2. In a heated wok or skillet add oil, stir fry garlic and onions till browned. Add the carrots, bamboo shoots., and green beans 2 minutes. Add the curry and coat at everything.
3. Add the pineapple and shrimp. Cook for 2 minutes.
4. In a plate spread the cooked rice and put the content of the pan on it. Top with coriander and scallions.

* You could add the coriander and scallions while cooking everything too. It would be best to use individual dishes when distributing everything. This is a 2-3 person meal depending on the size plate we wish to eat.

# Telay Thai-Steamed Fishes and Chili Sauce

1/2 lb shrimp
1/2 lb scallops
1/2 lb fish of choice
1/2 lb of squid (cleaned and sliced include tentacles)
8 to 16 oz of rice vermicelli
« lime (juiced) or 1/3 cup lime juice
5 to 1o cloves garlic (crushed)
1/3 cup chili sauce
1 stalk lemon grass (crushed or chopped)
or 1 tbsp citronella oil or powder
2 tsp. white or brown sugar

1. Steam sea food in a steamer. Steam them separately. Fish 3 to 4 minutes or more. Squid 3 to 4 minutes or more. Scallops 3 to 5 minutes or more. Shrimp 2 to 3 minutes.
2. Boil vermicelli to package directions.
3. In a wok or skillet heat the oil and fry the garlic and lemon grass till fragrant. Discard both.
4. Add fish, lime juice, sugar, chili sauce. Cook to coat 2 minutes.
5. Make a bed with the vermicelli and pour the Talay on top. 76

# Pla Jian-Deep Fried Fish with Ginger Garlic Sauce

1 lb fish of choice
3 cloves garlic (crushed)
2 tbsp lime juice
1 tbsp red pepper flakes
1 tsp. brown sugar
1 tbsp flour
10 cloves garlic (crushed)
1 inch piece ginger (julienne)
4 scallions
2 red chilies (sliced)

1.  Marinate the fish with 2 cloves of garlic, lime juice, red pepper flakes, and sugar for 15 minutes. Coat with flour after words.
2.  In a wok or skillet, deep fry the fish till it is golden brown.
3.  In a small skillet add a little oil and fry the garlic, ginger, and red peppers.
4.  Place the fish in a dish and pour the sauce over it.

*  One could bake this in a oven or steam it for 20 minutes. If you choose not to fry anything, add it all in one cooking vessel and bake or steam.

# Pla Rad Prig-Fried Fish with Garlic and Chili Sauce

1 lb fish of choice
3 cloves garlic (crushed)
2 tbsp lime juice
1 tbsp red pepper flakes
1 tsp. brown sugar
1 tbsp flour
10 cloves garlic (crushed)
4 tbsp of chili paste

1. Marinate the fish with 2 cloves of garlic, lime juice, red pepper flakes, and sugar for 15 minutes. Coat with flour after words.
2. In a wok or skillet, deep fry the fish till it is golden brown.
3. In a hot wok or skillet add oil and fry the garlic till browned. Add the fish and chili sauce and cook for 2 minutes.

* Take caution a over cooked fish will fall apart, the meat must be white. When beep frying fish, the batter of coating turns golden brown.

# Chicken Stiuffed Squid in Green Curry

1 lb squid (Cleaned)
3/4 lb Chicken (ground)
1 tbsp Green curry paste
1 or 2 cans coconut milk
1/4 cup coriander leaves
3 scallions
4 tbsp lemon juice
2-3 tbsp fish sauce
1 tsp. red pepper flakes

1.  In a wok or skillet stir fry chicken meat and all the ingredients. sans squid, curry paste, and coconut milk. When cooked set it a side and let it cool.
2.  Clean the squid and stuff it with the chicken meat. Use a tsp. or pastry tube. (Or water ever tool you find that does the job). Put the tentacles on last.
3.  Heat a wok or skillet and add oil. Then add the curry and stir it around. Add the squid and cook it till done, maybe 3 to 4 minutes. Add the Coconut milk and bring to a boil.
4.  Distribute the squid and sauce evenly in serving dishes.

*   This is a wonderful dish I picked up in San Francisco. It amazes me of the similarity in Asian cooking, as Italian, to use seafood and meat in the same way.

# MYANMAR (BURMA)

# Balachong

1 tbsp shrimp paste
4 tbsp tamarind juice
2 tbsp vegetable oil
2 tsp. turmeric
1 tsp. paprika
2 tsp. red pepper flakes
1/2 cup shrimp powder
1/2 cup crispy fried onions
2 tbsp garlic (caramelized)

1. Fry 1 lb small onions, sliced, in oil and 1 tsp. turmeric. Brown
   the onions. Slice the garlic and caramelize it. Set aside.
2. Heat oil in a wok or skillet, Add paprika, turmeric, and red
   pepper flakes and fry for a moment.
3. Mix the shrimp paste and tamarind liquid together. To the wok
   add the shrimp powder, stir, then the shrimp/tamarind mixture.
   Stir fry for one minute.
4. Add the onions and garlic for a moment and remove from heat.
   Serve at room temperature.

* Instead of red pepper flakes, one could use a fresh red pepper,
and green one. When using balachong on meats dishes. Add
peppers to the dish.

# Sesame Satay

1 lb of chicken
1/2 to 1/3 cup of Sesame seems
1/2 cup of water
2 tbsp soy sauce
1 tbsp sesame oil
2 tsp. of lemon grass or citronella oil
3 or for cloves of garlic
1 tbsp curry powder.

1. Cut the chicken in 1 inch chunks and place them on a skewer.
2. In a blender of food processor add the sesame seeds, water, and other ingredients. Blend it till a smooth pastes forms.
3. Put the chicken skewers in a plate and pour over the marinade. Let it stand for several hours, turning over and integrating the meat with the puree.
4. Place then on a BBQ grill, or make them in a oven at 475 F. Cook till chicken turn white and turn over till it is done.

* If you are using a oven, you may want to add liquid smoke to the puree.

# Burmese Rice Dish

1 Cup of rice
1 pinch of saffron or Kasuba
1 tsp. cumin(grated)
1 tsp. ginger(grated)
1 clove of garlic
2 tbsp of unsweetened butter

1. Add the cup of rice to two cups of water and bring it to a boil.
2. add the saffron/Kasuba, spices, and garlic. Add the butter and stir.
3. After the water is absorbed in the rice. Cover it and steam it for 15 minutes.

# Golden Triangles

1 package of wonton or pastry wrappers.
2 potatoes (to be mashed)
1 tbsp Turmeric
1 tbsp curry powder

1. Cook the potatoes. Peel them and mash them. Ad a little milk if necessary. Keep the mash thick. Add the spices.
2. Stir and integrate the spices.
3. Take each pastry skin and add the potato mixture. Fold it over and seal it into a triangle.
4. Either deep fry at 3700F or bake it for twenty minute or till the pastry is golden brown.

\* This is also good with the puff pastry recipe. Use same method as triangle.

# Calabash Fingers

1 Calabash (sliced lengthwise 6 inches)
2/3 cup rice flour
3 tbsp glutinous rice flour
3 tbsp chick pea flour
1/4 tsp. turmeric
1/4 tsp. paprika
1 clove garlic (crushed)
1 slice ginger (julienne)
1 tbsp corn oil
1/2 cup of cold water

1. Take the calabash and slice it into strips as large as fingers. Put them aside.
2. Mix batter with the remaining ingredients. then set it aside for 1 hour.
3. Dip each calabash finger in batter and coat it well.
4. Heat a skillet or wok and add 1 inch of oil. Deep fry each calabash finger till they are golden brown.
5. Remove and drain, then top with Balachong if so desired.

* This batter can be used with any vegetable, or meat.

# Tok Tok Rolls

1 1/2-2 cups shredded Napa
½-1 cup bean sprouts.
2 carrots (shredded)
1 can bamboo shoots. (shredded)
2 or 3 rutabaga (shredded)
2 cans of baby shrimp
1/2 cup of soy sauce
8 oz cellophane noodles (soaked 10 minutes, cut into 3 inch pieces)
10 spring roll or Shanghai egg roll wrappers

1. Prepare the vegetables and noodles, then heat a wok or skillet
   and cook them. Add the Napa first, cook for 2 minutes. then
   the rutabaga, cook for 2 minutes. Then add the rest with the
   soy sauce and cook them a extra 2 minutes. Add the shrimp
   and noodles, cook 1 minute and set aside.
2. Add 1 to 2 tbsp. of the vegetables inside the spring roll skin,
   place one corner to the center, fold the other 2 sides and roll it
   up.
3. These should be placed in a steamer and steamed for 10 to 15
   minutes, or when the skin seems translucent.

* These could be dipped in soy sauce or Balachong.

# Crispy Lentil Fritters

1 cup lentils (any variety)
1 cup rice flour
1 onion (deiced)
1/2 cup mint (chopped)
1 or 2 chili peppers (Deiced)
1 tsp. ginger powder
1 tsp. baking powder

1. Soak lentils in water over night. They should be soft and ready for the food processor. Place them in and blend them to a paste. Remember to drain them first.
2. Mix the paste with rice flour and the remaining ingredients. in a bowl. Mix it thoroughly. Let it stand for 1 hour.
3. Make patties 2 inches thick, « inch diameter. Heat the woke or skillet, add oil and fry them till browned. Maybe three minutes on each side.

* Place them on a paper towel to drain.

# Fried Shrimp

1 or 1/2 lb shrimp (shelled and de-vein)
1/2 tsp. turmeric powder
1/2 onion (sliced)
2 cloves garlic (crushed)
1/4 to 1/2 inch ginger (sliced)
1 tsp. red chili flakes
1 tsp. paprika
1 tbsp fish sauce

1.  Marinade shrimp in turmeric for ten minutes.
2.  Coarsely chop the onion, garlic, ginger. Blend in the spices.
3.  In a hot wok or skillet add oil and fry the onion mixture until the is browned. Then add the fish sauce and mix it around, then add the shrimp and cook till they are pink.

\*   Other sea foods can be cooked with this mixture. Also vegetable dishes.

# Lima Bean Soup

1 cup peeled lima beans
1/4 tsp. turmeric
3 cups water
1 small onion
1 tbsp fish sauce
1/4 to « watercress
1lb fish fillet

1. Soak lima beans over night, then when they are soft, peel the skins off.
2. Add water to a pot, add the fish, and bring to a boil. Add onions fish sauce. Simultaneously, add lima beans and turmeric to a oiled skillet and fry for 5 minutes. Add it to the soup stock.
3. Cook the soup till the fish is white and flaky, add water cress to individual bowls and pour soup in it.

* Yellow lentils may be substituted.

# 12 Ingredients Soup

12 Ingredients
1 lb boneless chicken breast
1 lb shrimp (shelled and deviened)
1 lb pork (sliced thin)
16 oz chicken stock
1 tbsp shrimp sauce
1 onion (sliced)
2 cloves garlic (crushed)
2 ginger slices
1 cake tofu (cut to 1 inch squares)
18 oz tiger lily buds
1/2 shiitake mushrooms (soaked and sliced)
1 medium zucchinis (sliced)
2 scallions (sliced)

1. In separate pans cook the shrimp till pink, and pork till it is white. Shred the pork with a sharp knife.
2. Add chicken stock to a pot with chicken breastsp.p, and boil add adding the remaining ingredients.
3. When the chicken is cooked, add the pork and the shrimp. Stir it and serve.

*   One could save the scallions and add them as a garnish.

# Coconut Noodle Soup

3/4 lb to 1 lb chicken breast (sliced thin)
16 oz egg noodles (par boiled)
1 tsp. turmeric
1 tsp. cumin
1 tsp. ginger powder
2 cloves garlic (crushed)
16 oz coconut milk
4 oz fresh coriander leaves
1 onion (quartered and sliced)

1. Slice chicken thinly and in a wok, sauté with garlic and ginger. Use fresh ginger if preferred.
2. When chicken is just about done, add turmeric and cumin and cook 1 minute, then add the coconut milk.
3. When chicken is done add the noodles. Serve in separate bowls garnishing it with coriander and raw onions.

* This will be equally good with shrimp.

# BEEF

## Curried Beef

1lb beef (sliced thin)
1/2 tsp. turmeric powder
1/2 tsp. paprika powder
1 tsp. ginger (minced)
1 tbsp cilantro
« tsp. red pepper powder
1 onion (sliced)
2 tomatoes (chopped)
3 cups water

1. In a bowl, combine all the ingredients. and integrate thoroughly. Let it stand 1 hour.
2. Heat a wok or skillet, add 2 tbsp. of oil. Add the beef mixture. Cook till beef is slightly browned.
3. Add the water and cook till it is reduced to half. If more cooking time is needed add more water.

*   Adding coconut milk is also recommended

# Satay Beef

1 lb beef chunks (« by « inch)
1/4 to 1/3 cup of Sesame seems
1/2 cup of water
2 tbsp soy sauce
1 tbsp sesame oil
2 tsp. of lemon grass or citronella oil
3 or for cloves of garlic
1 tsp. turmeric
1 tsp. cumin
1 tsp. paprika

1. In a blender of food processor add the sesame seeds, water, and other ingredients. Blend it till a smooth pastes forms.
2. Mix all the ingredients. in a bowl and marinade 30 minutes.
3. Thread the meat mixture on skewers. Wet skewers first.
4. Light coals in the grill and allow them to become white hot. Add the beef on the grill and cook till browned through.

# Burmese Beef

1 lb beef (sliced thin)
1/2 tsp. turmeric
1 tbsp soy sauce
4 cloves garlic (sliced)
2 tbsp Balachong

1.  Marinade beef with turmeric and soy sauce. Then heat wok or skillet. Add oil, then cook the beef with the garlic till almost browned.
2.  Add balachong and cook the beef all the way through or to desire.

*   Balachong can be made mild by using sweet peppers.

# Beef Kabot

1 1/2 lb beef (sliced thin)
1 tsp. turmeric
1 tsp. cardamom (powdered)
1 tsp. ginger (minced)
1 red pepper (hot or sweet)
1 green pepper (hot or sweet)
1 tomato (sliced)
1 onion (sliced)
1 tbsp mint leaves
2 tbsp red wine or sherry
1 tbsp soy sauce
1/4 cup cilantro leaves

1. Marinade beef in turmeric, soy sauce, and red wine. Let it sit 1 hour.
2. Clean and slice peppers and vegetables. Heat wok or skillet and add oil. Fry the onions and peppers till soft. Add the beef, mint, and cardamom.
3. Stir fry till meat is browned and completely cooked. Add cilantro leaves and steam for a minute then serve.

# Beef Mint Kababs

1 1/2 lb beef (1 inch x 1 inch)
1/2 tsp. turmeric
1/2 tsp. cumin
1 tbsp soy sauce
1 onion (quartered)
1 green pepper (sliced)
1 red pepper (sliced)
1 tomato (sliced)
1/2 cup mint (sliced)

1. Marinade beef in soy sauce, cumin, and turmeric, and the mint. Let it stand 1 hour.
2. Intermittently, string meat and vegetables on bamboo skewers. Then light the coals in a grill till they are white hot.
3. Place them on the grill and turn them as each side browns. Cook all the way through making sure meat is well done.

* One could ad a little sherry or rice wine to the marinade.

# Lemon Grass Beef

1 1/2 lb beef (sliced)
1/2 tsp. turmeric
1/2 tsp. cumin
1/2 tsp. paprika
1 tbsp soy sauce
1 stalk lemon grass (ground or sliced)
2 potatoes (cooked and quartered)
1 can coconut milk
1/2 cup cilantro

1. Marinade the beef in turmeric, cumin, paprika, and soy sauce.
2. Heat wok or skillet and oil then add the lemon grass, cook for 1 minute, then discard.
3. Ad the beef, and stir fry till brown. Add the potatoes, then cook till done. Add coconut milk and heat it till it almost boils. Add cilantro leaves and serve.

# PORK

## Pineapple Pork

2 lbs boneless pork (cubed 2 x 2 inches)
2 tsp. ginger (minced)
1 tbsp paprika
2 tsp. red pepper flakes (optional)
1 onion (chopped)
2 or 3 cloves garlic (crushed)
2 tbsp fish sauce
1 cup or 8 oz of pineapple cubes
2 cups of water

1. In a bowl mix all the ingredients. together, omitting water, and allow it to sit for 20 minutes.
2. Heat wok or skillet, add oil, then transfer pork mixture to the heated vessel.
3. Stir fry a moment and then add water and cook for perhaps 45 minutes. Allow water to boil till it seem as if it is reduced to 1/2 cup.

*  It is more important to make sure the pork is cooked, if you wish add less water.

# Pork with Mango Chutney

1 1/2 lbs pork (cubed 2 x 2 inches)
1 ginger (sliced, about 1 inch)
2 cloves garlic (crushed)
2 tsp. red pepper flakes
1/2 tsp. turmeric
1/2 tsp. cumin
1 tsp. shrimp paste
2 tsp. shrimp sauce
1/4 to 1/2 half cup mango chutney
1« cups water

1. Take onion, garlic, and ginger, place it in a blender or food processor and make a paste out of it.
2. Heat a wok or skillet and fry the paste, red pepper flakes, turmeric, cumin, and fry till it has a red/brown appearance. Add shrimp paste and shrimp sauce and cook 2 minutes.
3. Add the pork and chutney. Fry the mixture till the pork is browned.
4. Add the water and cook for 30 minutes or more. The sauce should thicken and be greatly reduced.

*   To make chutney get 1 green mango and slice it thin, 1/4 cup sugar, ¼ cup of cider vinegar, and salt. Cook for 10 minutes covered. 10 minutes uncovered. When mango is soft eat it or store it.

# Pork Cutlet with Vegetables

1 lb pork chops
1/2 cup rice flour
1 tbsp glutinous rice flour
1 tsp. turmeric
1 tbsp soy sauce
1 tsp. cold water
1/2 cup cold water
1 chayote (sliced thin)
1 small Napa cabbage (Shredded)
2 cloves garlic (crushed)

1. Mix batter using 1 tsp. of soy sauce. Beat until smooth.
2. Marinade the pork in remaining soy sauce. Ad a little salt or sugar if so desired.
3. In one heated wok or skillet, add oil. Dip the pork in batter and fry. Each side should be a golden brown.
4. Simultaneously, in another wok or skillet, heat, add oil and fry the garlic. Then add Napa and Chayote and stir fry till they are soft, yet firm.
5. In each platter add some Napa, chayote mixture, then place on the pork chop.

# Rangoon Smoked Pork

1 1/2 lb pork
2 tbsp soy sauce
1 tbsp sherry or rice wine
1 tsp. turmeric
1 tbsp cumin
1 tbsp paprika
1 tbsp ginger
1 tbsp sugar

1. In a bowl marinade all the ingredients. Let it stand 30 minutes or more.
2. Heat coals with hickory chips in a grill, or add to the marinade liquid smoke particularly if you are not grilling over coals.
3. Place each on a grill and cook till brown. It is the same when using a stove top grill, cook till browned.

*   The India breads I mentioned can be served with this as well as other recipes in the Myanmar selection

# Pork Spareribs

1 1/2 lbs pork spare ribs (cut into 1 inch cubes)
2 egg yolks (beaten)
2 tbsp soy sauce
2 scallions or leeks (sliced)
1 tsp. star anise (ground)
2 cups oil

1. After chopping the spare ribs place them in a bowl with the beaten egg yolks and marinate for 2 hours.
2. In a deep fryer or wok, heat oil to 350o F. Add the ribs and fry them till they are browned.
3. Remove the ribs and drain them in the basket or on paper towels.
4. Remove oil from the wok, or get a clean skillet or wok and heat it. Add 2 tbsp. of oil and stir fry the star anise and scallions for a minute. Add the soy sauce and ribs and stir fry 1 more minute.

*   If you have five spice powder, use it, since the contents has star anise and other spices that will make it a even tastier dish.

# CHICKEN

## Chili Chicken

1 or 2 chicken breasts (boned and deiced)
1 or 2 eggs (separated
4 cloves garlic (sliced)
1 inch ginger (sliced)
1/2 onion (sliced)
1 small green chili pepper (sliced)
2 tbsp soy sauce
2 stalks of scallion (sliced)
1 tsp. coriander

1. Beat egg yolk and marinate the chicken with it. Let it stand 39 minutes.
2. Heat wok or skillet, add oil. Fry garlic and ginger for 30 seconds. Add the chicken and stir fry 2 minutes.
3. Add the soy sauce, chili peppers, and onion, and stir fry for a moment. Then add the egg white. After the egg whitens, add scallions and coriander.

* Along with garlic and ginger, it would be a good idea to add a little lemon grass.

# Spiced Chicken Wing

6 to 8 chicken wings
1 tsp. turmeric
1 tsp. paprika
1 tsp. ginger
2 tsp. shrimp paste
2 cloves garlic (crushed)
1 onion (sliced)
1 green chili

1. If desired, cut off chicken wing tips. Marinate the chicken wings in turmeric for 10 minutes.
2. Blend the onion, garlic, ginger, and chili into a fine paste. Heat a wok or skillet, add oil. Add the shrimp paste and chili paste and stir for a moment. Add the wings and cook till they are browned.
3. Heat a broiler, or charcoal grill. Place the wings in a broiler pan. or on the grill. Cook them till they are done.

* This could become a curry by adding 2 cup of water and cumin. Reduce the liquid till thickened. Coconut can substitute water. But do not reduce, just heat it, do not boil.

# Barbecued Chicken

1 2-3 lb chicken
1 tbsp fermented tofu
2 tsp. honey
1 tbsp lime juice
2 tbsp soy sauce
1 tsp. shrimp paste
1 tsp. paprika
1 tsp. oil

1. Cut the chicken in half, discard loose skin and fat.
2. In a bowl mix fermented tofu, honey, lime juice, soy sauce, shrimp paste, paprika, and oil. Make a paste.
3. Coat the entire chicken with the marinade and let it stand for 2 hours.
4. Heat a broiler or grill and place the chicken on a broiler rack or grill. Cook 20 minutes on each side or till done.

# Chicken in Red Bean Paste

1 1/2 lb chicken (boneless and cubed « x « inch)
1 tsp. turmeric
2 cloves garlic
2 ginger slices
2 tbsp red bean sauce
1 tbsp soy sauce
1/2 tsp. sesame chili oil
1 tsp. rice wine
1 leaf lettuce
« cucumber (sliced)

1. Cut the chicken in half. Marinate the chicken in turmeric for 1-2 hours.
2. Mix the red bean sauce, soy sauce sesame chili oil, and rice wine in a bowl.
3. Heat the wok and stir fry the chicken till it is whitened. Then add the red bean sauce mix. Coat it well and allow it to thicken.
4. In a plate, add the lettuce. Place the cooked chicken on top and surround the out side with layers of cucumber.

# Rangoon Smoked Tea Duck

1 Duck (halved)
1 tsp. turmeric
1 tsp. cumin
1 tsp. paprika
1 tsp. ginger
4 tbsp soy sauce
2 tbsp red bean sauce
1 tbsp Burmese tea or Oolong Tea

1. Halve the duck and either remove the skin and fat, or boil it for twenty minutes.
2. In a bowl coat the duck with soy sauce and red bean sauce marinate it for 2 hours.
3. Heat the coal till they are white hot. Add hickory chips and Burmese tea. Immediately add the duck and cook it till it is done.

* There are many Asian teas one could use. If you choose to smoke the duck directly it may take a while to cook.

# Chicken in Pickled Mustard Greens

1 1/2 lb chicken (sliced)
1 to 2 cups fermented mustard greens
4 cloves garlic (crushed
1 tsp. ginger
1 onion (sliced)
2 tbsp soy sauce
2 tbsp fish sauce
1/2 tsp. black pepper
2 scallions (sliced)
4 cups chicken stock

1.  Clean the mustard green if necessary. Cut into 1 inch thick slices.
2.  Clean the skin and fat off of the chicken is necessary.
3.  In a sauce pan, bring the chicken stock to a boil. Add the rest of the ingredients. except the scallions.
4.  Add the chicken and mustard greens and cook till they are done.

*   Add more water or chicken stock if necessary. You could make mustard green preserves by adding 1 bunch of mustard greens. 1 tsp. turmeric. 2 tsp. red chili flakes. 2 tsp. brown sugar.! cup of beer and ferment for three days.

# LAMB

## Barbecued Lamb Chops

1 lb lamb chop (sliced)
1/2 tsp. turmeric
1/2 tsp. salt
1/2 tsp. pepper
2 tbsp lemon juice
2 tbsp soy sauce
1 tbsp honey
1 tsp. cumin
1 tsp. paprika

1. Slice the lamb into slender chunks and marinade in turmeric, salt, and pepper for 15 minutes. Thread on bamboo skewers.
2. mix the marinade ingredients. and set it aside
3. In a broiler or on a grill cook the lamb chops till they are brown. Baste them as they are about to be done.

# Lamb Curry

1 lb lamb ribs (cut 1 « inch lengths)
1/2 tsp. turmeric
1/2 tsp. paprika
1/2 tsp. cumin
1 tbsp fish sauce
2 yellow onions
2 tbsp rice vinegar
3 cup of water
2 potatoes (cooked, peeled, cut into 8ths)
1/2 cup cilantro

1. In a bowl place lamb chops, and marinate with turmeric, paprika, and cumin. Then add fish sauce. Let it stand 1 hour.
2. In a wok or skillet, fry the onions till translucent, add the lamb and vinegar. Cover it with water and boil it till it thickens.
3. Add the potatoes, cook for 1 minute. Then top with the cilantro. Serve.

\* The potatoes can be cooked with the lamb if preferred.

# Barbecued Leg of Lamb with Yogurt

10 lb leg of lamb (cut into 1 inch cubes)
2 1/2 cups of plain yogurt
1/2 tsp. salt
1 tbsp turmeric
1 tbsp paprika
1/4 cup cumin
1/2 tsp. nutmeg
1/2 tsp. cloves (powdered)
1/2 tsp. bay leaves (powdered)
5 tbs. sesame oil

1. In a bowl mix all of the ingredients. Integrate well and leave to marinate over night.
2. In a grill heat the coals till white. Place the lamb chunks on skewers and cook them till they are browned. Possibly 10 minutes on each side.

\* Stove top grills and broiling is a acceptable alternative. Use liquid smoke for a authenticated taste.

# Festival Rice I

2 cups of glutinous rice
1 tsp. ginger
1/2 cup roasted peanuts.
1/3 cup toasted sesame seeds
1/4 cup of coconut slices (1 inch long)
1/3 cup peanut oil

1. Soak the rice for one hour. Then Heat a wok and add the oil then ginger for a few seconds. Then add the rice with 4 cup of water. Let it cook till rice has absorbed the water. Stir the rice a few times during cooking.
2. Let the rice stand for ten minutes off the heat. Transfer it to a food processor. Puree the rice to a smooth texture.
3. Add the peanuts., sesame seeds, and coconut to the rice. Integrate it well and serve at room temperature.

—

# Festival Rice II

2 cups rice
1 lb chicken breast (sliced)
2 cans chicken stock
1 tsp. cinnamon
5 bay leaves
1/2 cup of raisins or currants
1 1/2 tsp. ghee

1. Add two cups of rice and 4 cups of chicken stock to a pot and bring it to a boil. Add the chicken beast and stir.
2. Add cinnamon, bay leaves, raisins and ghee. Stir it around a bit, then cover the top, lift it once in a while to prevent over flow and pressure.
3. After 20 minutes or more, the rice should absorb the liquid. Take it of the heat and let it sit 10 to 20 minutes.

# SEAFOOD

## Fish Cake

1 1/2 lbs fish (white fish)
1/2 tsp. paprika
1/2 tsp. ginger (Julienne)
1/2 tsp. turmeric
4 cloves garlic
1 tbsp fish sauce
1/4 cup peanut oil

1. In a food processor, or mortar place ginger and garlic. Process them till they are a smooth paste. Cut the fish in 1« inch slices and add that to the food processor. Blend to a smooth paste.
2. Add the spices and fish sauce. Blend it well in to the fish mix.
3. Prepare the fish cakes by making a round patty. Heat wok or skillet and add the oil. Fry them till they are a golden brown, 3 minutes on each side should do it.

* Oil fingers a bit so fish cakes don't stick.

# Fish Cake Salad

Fish cake recipe as above
1 onion (sliced)
1 small green pepper (sliced)
1 scallion (sliced)
1/2 cup crispy fried onions (see balachong recipe)
1 small cucumber (quartered and sliced)
2 tbsp lime juice
2 tsp. fish sauce
1/2 cup of coriander (sliced)

1. Instead of deep frying the fish cake, boil them in « cup of water. 2 minutes each side should do it. Cool them and slice them in 1 inch strips.
2. Toss the salad with the fish cakes and add the lemon and fish sauce. Top it with the crispy onions and any oil from them.
3. Another way is to arrange the vegetables, fish cakes in the middle, surrounded by cucumbers, then layer the vegetables on top, saving the crispy onions for the top layer. Fish cakes will be delicate, do not toss the salad to vigorously.

# Fried Calamari

1 lb fresh squid (cleaned and cut in « inch circles)
2/3 cup rice flour
3 tbsp glutinous rice flour
1 tbsp wheat flour
1/4 tsp. turmeric
1/2 tsp. salt
1/2 cup water
2 cup oil

1.  Prepare batter by mixing rice flours, wheat flour, turmeric, salt, and water. Integrate well and allow it to stand 30 minutes.
2.  Heat oil in a skillet or wok to 350o F and dip each squid slice in the batter and deep fry.
3.  They should be slightly browned, do not over cook, remove with a wire whisk or slotted spoon. Place them on paper towels and allow them to drain.

*   serve this on a bed of lettuce surrounded by cucumbers. They can be dipped in soy sauce, mixed with a bit of sesame oil.

# Crab Dumpling

8 oz canned crab meat
1 tsp. turmeric
1 tsp. paprika
2 cloves garlic (crushed)
1/2 onion (chopped)
1/4 cup cilantro (chopped)
8 oz cream cheese (softened)
wonton wrappers.

1. In a blender or food processor add the ingredients., mix till all the mixture is integrated.
2. Place a tbsp. filled with the mixture in a won ton or dumpling wrapper.
3. Boil water in a steamer and steam then for 10 minutes. Or deep fry them in 4 cup of oil, 350o F.

\* It would be ideal for hot and spicy fans to top it with balachong.

# Mixed Seafood with Vegetables

2 lbs variety of seafood
1 tsp. turmeric
1 tsp. cumin
1 tsp. paprika
1 tsp. coriander
1 onion (deiced)
3 or 4 bay leaves
1/4 to 1/2 cup cilantro (chopped)
1 egg plant (cubed)
1 daikon (sliced)
1 yellow squash (sliced)
2 carrots (sliced)
3 potatoes (cooked)
« cup tamarind juice
4 cups of water

1.  Heat a pan and add 2 tbsp. of oil. Add the spices, onions, and bay leaves.
2.  Add the water, tamarind juice, and vegetables. Boil them till they are slightly soft.
3.  Add the fish and boil till the fish is done. Add the cilantro.

*  Also Use fish fillets, scallops, shrimp, clams.

# Shrimp Salad

1 lb shrimp (peeled and de-veined)
1/2 tsp. turmeric
2 tsp. garlic oil
2 tbsp lime juice
1/4 cup crispy onions
1 onion (sliced)
1 head romaine lettuce
1 cucumber (sliced)
2 carrots (julienne)
2 or 3 scallions
« cup cilantro

1. boil shrimp in water till they are pink. Set them aside and allow them to cool.
2. Add the shrimp and vegetables, saving scallions and cilantro till last, toss and mix well.
3. Mix the turmeric, garlic oil, and lime juice to make a dressing and toss the salad again.
4. Add the cilantro and scallions atop.

\* Garlic oil can be made by adding 8 cloves of sliced garlic to hot oil in a wok and caramelize. Heat wok then add oil and garlic.

# Burmese Sweet and Sour Shrimp

1 lb fresh shrimp (peeled and de-veined)
2/3 cup rice flour
3 tbsp glutinous rice flour
1 tbsp wheat flour
1/4 tsp. turmeric
1/2 tsp. salt
1/2 cup water
2 cup oil
4oz pineapple juice
1/2 cup honey
1/2 cup rice wine vinegar
1 tbsp soy sauce
2 tbsp rice flour

1.  Prepare batter by mixing rice flours, wheat flour, turmeric, salt, and water. Integrate well and allow it to stand 30 minutes.
2.  Heat oil in a skillet or wok to 350o F and dip each shrimp slice in the batter and deep fry. They should be slightly browned, do not over cook, remove with a wire whisk or slotted spoon. Place them on paper towels and allow them to drain.
3.  Then in a wok or skillet, mix the pineapple juice, honey, rice vinegar, honey, and rice flour. cook till this thickens and mix in the shrimp for a moment and coat them.

# NOODLES

## Panthay Noodles

1 lb boneless chicken (cubed 1 inch)
1 tsp. turmeric
1 tsp. cumin
1 tsp. paprika
1 tsp. red chili flakes
3 tbsp soy sauce
2 clove garlic (minced)
1 onion (sliced)
1/2 lb ripe tomatoes (sliced)
1 lb egg spaghetti (9 Italian alternate)
2 scallions (sliced)
1 small Napa cabbage (shredded)
2 tbsp lime juice (lemon is ok)

1.  Marinate the chicken in 2 tbsp. of soy sauce, turmeric, paprika, and cumin. Let stand 30 minutes.
2.  In a large pot boil water, add the spaghetti and cook for twenty minutes. Strain in a colander when done.
3.  Simultaneously heat wok or skillet and add the oil, onions and garlic. After a short moment add tomatoes and chicken. stir fry till chicken is almost dome. Add the broth and cook for 20 minutes.
4.  Place spaghetti in a bowl and add 1 tbsp. of soy sauce, mix well.
5.  Place spaghetti in each plate and place the curried chicken atop. Then garnish it with scallions, lime juice, cabbage, and red chili flakes.

# Street Market Noodles

1 Duck (roasted and de-boned)
1 lb spaghetti (#9 Italian) or Egg Noodles
1/2 tsp. turmeric
1/2 tsp. paprika
1/2 tsp. cumin
1/2 tsp. coriander
3 tbsp soy sauce
2 tbsp lemon
2 tbsp garlic oil
2 scallions (chopped)

1. Marinate duck with lemon juice, turmeric, cumin, paprika, and coriander. Let it stand 1 hour.
2. Place the duck in a broiler or grill. Cook 45 minutes or till done.
3. Let the duck cool a bit, then de-bone and shred it making sure it is not in strands.
4. Boil the water and cook the spaghetti, 20 minutes to the most. Strain in colander when done.
5. In a hot wok or skillet, ad a table spoon of oil and the duck. Add the garlic oil and stir fry for 2 minutes. Add 1 tbsp. of soy sauce and mix well.
6. In a bowl pour the spaghetti and add the soy sauce. Place in plate with the duck as a topping, then ad the scallions.

# Mandalay Nungyl Noodles

1 lb chicken (cubed)
8 to 16 oz wide rice noodles
1/2 tsp. turmeric
1/2 tsp. paprika
1/2 tsp. cumin
3 tbsp soy sauce
2 tbsp besan
1 onion (sliced)
2 tbsp garlic oil
1 tbsp lemon juice

1. Marinate chicken in spices, 2 tbsp. of soy sauce, and lemon juice. let it stand 30 minutes.
2. Roast besan in a frying pan, dry, and toast till brown, do not scorch.
3. Cook the noodles in boiling water, maybe seven minutes or to el dente. Drain in colander.
4. Heat wok or skillet, add a little oil, the place the chicken in. Add the garlic oil and besan, and stir fry till chicken is done.
5. Ad soy sauce to the noodles and place them in a plate with the chicken mixture atop.

# Shan Rice Noodle

1 lb chicken (sliced)
8 oz thick rice noodles
1 tsp. turmeric
1 tsp. cumin
1 tsp. Paprika
3 tbsp soy sauce
1 tsp. toasted sesame seeds
1 tbsp ground peanut (roasted)
4 tsp. toasted sesame oil

1. Marinate chicken in 2 tbsp soy sauce and spices, allow to stand 30 minutes.
2. Heat wok or skillet and add oil, stir fry the chicken till it is whitened.
3. Cook rice noodles by boiling them in a pot of water seven minutes. Drain and reserve.
4. Add the rice noodles, with the chicken, mix well then add the soy sauce and sesame oil. Mix for a few seconds. Add the sesame seeds and sesame seeds and mix it. Divide it in platters and top it with ground peanuts.

# BHUTAN
## (Land of the Thunder Dragon)

# Pork Fing

1 package cellophane noodles
1 medium onion
1 tomato (sliced)
4 oz stick sweet butter
1 /2 pounds pork shoulder 1 inch Cubes
1/2 cup water
3 green chili peppers (julienne)
Salt
black pepper

1. Soften the bean threads in a bowl of boiling water for two minutes.
2. Drain and cut into 6-inch lengths. Chop the onion coarsely.
3. Chop the tomato and. Chop the onion coarsely.
4. Melt the butter in a large saucepan. Add the onion, tomato, pork, and water and simmer over low heat until tender, about 1 hour and 30 minutes.
5. Add the bean threads, chili peppers, and salt and pepper to taste and simmer until heated through, about 5-10 minutes.

# Tphoem

1 large garlic clove [about 1/6 ounce, 5g], peeled
Fresh ginger, peeled and cut into a 3/4-inch [2cm] cube
4 oz stick sweet
1 pound boneless beef chuck (cubed)
1 tsp. salt
2 medium fresh green chili peppers
11/3 cups fresh oyster mushrooms
Freshly ground black pepper

1. Chop the onion, the garlic, and ginger set aside.
2. Melt the butter in a large saucepan. Add the beef, onion, water, and salt and simmer over low heat until just tender.
3. Add the garlic, ginger, and remaining ingredients. and cook until the mushrooms are tender, about 10 minutes.

# Phaksha Pa

1 medium (peeled and quartered )
Fresh ginger, peeled and cubed
1 medium daikon or white radish
4 oz sweet butter
1 pound boneless pork chops (cut into strips )
1/2 cup water
2 tbsp. chili powder
2 tbsp salt
3 large heads bok choy (cut leaves cut into 1/2-inch strips)
6 ounces dried pork , (cut into 3 by 1/2 inch chunks)
1 large fresh green chili pepper, (seeded and cut into strips)

1.  Chop the onion. Set aside. Slice the ginger into cubes.
2.  Melt the butter in a large frying pan. Add the pork shoulder,
    onion, daikon, water, chili powder, and salt and simmer over
    low heat until the pork is tender.
3.  Meanwhile, scald the bok choy in a large pot of boiling water
    until tender, about 5 minutes. Drain.
4.  Add the ginger, bok choy, fried pork, and chili pepper to the
    stew and simmer over low heat until heated through, 5 to 10
    minutes.

Edit 1

# Kewa Phagsha (Spicy Pork With Potatoes)

1 ½ of pork chops
2 potatoes peeled.
3 green chilies.
1 onion.
1/2 tsp. chili powder
3 cloves of garlic (crushed)
1 piece of ginger (finely chopped)
1/2 tbsp canola oil.

1.  Chop pork into large chunks. Add about 1 cup of water in a sauce pan. Add pork and a bit of salt and boil for about 20 minutes (Pork should be thoroughly cooked till soft ).
2.  Cut potatoes lengthwise into 6 or 8 pieces each.
3.  Cut chilies lengthwise into 2 pieces each. Add chili, potato and onion and 1/2 tsp. of canola oil.
4.  Cook until potato is mostly cooked. Add the remaining ingredients. and cook for 3-4 minutes. Stir. pepper or coriander seasoning to taste.

# Jasha Maroo (Minced Chicken)

1 chicken
2 tbsp. of vegetable oil
2 cloves garlic (crushed)
1 onion (sliced)
1 tomato (chopped)
3 green chilies (cut into small pieces) or use chili powder
1 tsp. salt

1. Cut chicken in very small pieces and place in a saucepan and add water and 2 tbsp. oil and bring to a boil.
2. Add garlic, salt and ginger. Lower heat slightly and boil for another 5-10 minutess stirring occasionally. The dish should have some liquid when you're done. Garnish with

# Ema Datshi

8 oz/250g of chilies (green and of medium hotness)
1 onion chopped lengthwise
2 tomatoes
8 oz/250g Fetta cheese or goat cheese
5 cloves of garlic, finely crushed
3 leaves of coriander
2 tsp. vegetable oil

1. Cut chilies lengthwise. In to strips. These could be green or red.
2. Placer the chilies and chopped onions in a pot of water (approx. 400 ml). Add 2 tsp. vegetable oil. Then boil in medium heat for about 10 minutes.
3. Add tomato and garlic and boil for another 2 mins. Add cheese and let it remain for 2-3 minutes.
4. Finally add coriander and turn off the heat. Stir. Keep it closed for 2 mins.

# Kewa Datsphi (Potatoes 'N' Cheese)

4 Large Potatoes
1/3 cup of cheese, (Feta or hard ricotta)
1/4 cup of chopped red onions
1 tbsp oil
1 tsp. salt 1/2 tsp. chili powder

1. Cut potatoes into lengthwise pieces. Put the potatoes with oil and salt in a pot. Brown them and add water to cover. Cook till done
2. Cut the cheese into small pieces (if not packaged already) and when the potatoes are almost cooked, add the cheese. Add some chopped onions and tomatoes and the chili powder.

The Bhutanese serve some soothing side dishes like this one:

## Burmese Garnish

1 seedless cucumber
1 medium red onion
1/2 cup crumbled farmer cheese [feta or hard ricotta)_
1 green chili pepper
Salt and freshly ground black pepper

1. Chop onions fine, and dice the onions. These should be very thin.
2. Green Chili Peppers should be sliced length wise.
3. In a bowl add the ingredients. and mix well.

# Hapai Hantue Buckwheat Dumplings with Bok Choy and Poppy Seed Filling

Filling
1 large head bok choy
2 tbsp. poppy seeds
1 tsp. Chinese Szechuan peppercorns or Chili peppers
2 cloves garlic
Fresh ginger, peeled and cut into a 3/4-inch cubes
1 small red onion
1/2 cup crumbled farmer cheese [
1 tsp. chili powder
1/4 tsp. salt
4 oz unsalted butter [4 ounces, 110g]

Dough
2 cups all-purpose flour
1 cup buckwheat flour
1 cup water
All-purpose flour, for dusting

1.  To make the filling, cook the bok choy in a pot of boiling water for 5 minutes. Drain and squeeze dry.
2.  Pulverize the poppy seeds and peppercorns with a spice or coffee grinder.
3.  Chop the garlic and ginger.
4.  Add the onion and chop finely, Add the bok choy, poppy seed mixture, cheese, chili powder, and salt.
5.  Melt the butter in a skillet over medium heat,.
6.  To make the dough, combine the two flours in the a bowl of a food processor fitted with the mixing blade. With the motor running pour the water through the feed tube and process until the dough forms a ball. Dust the ball with flour.
7.  Cut the dough into 8 pieces, dust with flour, and wrap 7 pieces in plastic wrap to prevent drying out.
8.  Roll out the dough to make. Flour the surface so the dough doesn't stick.

With a rolling pin make 4 by 2 inch [10 by 5cm] rectangles. Place 1 tsp. of the filling in the center of each rectangle. Brush the edges lightly with water and fold the rectangles over to make squares, pressing the edges to seal them well.

9. Cook the dumplings in batches in a saucepan or steamer of boiling water until tender, 7 to 8 minutes. Drain them in a colander or wired catcher—Be careful not to break them.

Edit 2

# Kamrupi Biriyani and Vegetable Fry-

3 cups of basmati or jasmine rice
8 oz Green peas
1/ tsp. turmeric powder
6-8 Green cardamom(cyrushed)
20 or more halved cashews
4 Black cardamom (crsahed)
2 cloves garlic
10-5 Whole cloves
1 knob of ginger (cubed)
4 Chicken breasts
Coriander leaves
One red or yellow large onion
1 small Eggplant (cubed)
8 oz broccoli flowerets
1 large Potato (parboiled, not soft)

1. Cook the rice to divide in two portions: 6 to 8 cups of water to 3 cups of rice
   (a) 3/4 as plain white rice; add a little oil (1-2 t. oil), add the green and black cardamoms. Add cashews—add water as appropriate, Cook till rice is cooked.
   (b) 1/4 as yellow rice; add a little oil (1 t. oil), than add 4 whole cloves add the turmeric. When the rice is done, add to each plate, ½ white, ½ yellow.
2. Preparation of ingredients.:
   (c) chop a potion of coriander, then slice the ginger; and cube or slice into small pieces. Chop the garlic; crush 4 green and 2 black cardamom together. Slice the onions. Open a can of peas, do not mix all the ingredients yet.
3. Preparation of Vegetable: Heat up at frying pan or wok, add two tablespoons of oil. Then add all the prepared vegetables. Cook till hot and degree of tenderness.

4. Preparation of Kamrupi Biriyani:
   In a separate frying pan heat at a low temperature and add oil, the add the chicken and cook till done. Then transfer to the vegetable pan. Add direction 2 ingredients and mix well. Place on top of rice on individual dishes.

# CAMBODIA

# Lemon Grass Curry Sauce

1/3 cup lemon grass (sliced)
4 cloves garlic
1 tsp. galangal
1 tsp. ground turmeric
1 tsp. cinnamon
1 Thai/ red chili
3 shallots.
3 1/2 cups coconut milk
3 Kafir lime leaves
1 shrimp paste

1.  Puree together the lemon grass, garlic, cinnamon, galangal, turmeric, peppers and shallots. In a food processor or blender.
2.  Bring the coconut milk to a simmer and add the pureed ingredients., lime leaves, and salt and boil gently, stirring constantly, for about 5 minutes on low heat. stirring often, for about 30 minutes, or until lime leaves are tender and the sauce is creamy. Remove the leaves before serving. To prepare one portion, pour 1/2 cup of this curry sauce into a shallow sauce panl or a wok.

# MEAT

## Aioan Chua Noeung Phset Kretni: Stir Fried Chicken with Mushrooms

6 dried Chinese mushrooms
1 small roasting chicken
4 cloves garlic, crushed
1/2 tsp. finely grated fresh ginger
2 tbsp. oil
1 cup water
2 tsp.s sugar
2 tbsp. chopped fresh coriander leaves

1. Soak mushrooms in hot water for 30 minutes. Squeeze dry, cut off and discard stems, cut caps into quarters.
2. Slice chicken into small pieces. Do not de-bone.
3. Fry garlic and ginger in the hot oil or oil for a few seconds, then add chicken and stir fry until meat is white and leaves the bone.
4. Add mushrooms, water and sugar, cover and simmer until chicken is cooked. Sprinkle with chopped coriander and serve with rice.

# Khmer Beef

1 pound beef
2 red peppers
4 stalks lemongrass—(sliced thin)
6 lime leaves or the peel of 1 lime
1 8 oz can of Pineapples.
4 cloves garlic
1 tsp. galangal or
A few slices of galangal t
1 tbsp. oyster sauce
2 tbsp. sugar
1 pinch salt
2 cups water

1. Cut beef into thin slices and thread on skewers.
2. Process or blend the red peepers, lemon grass, lime leaves, garlic and galangal into a paste.
3. Combine the paste with the pineapples, oyster sauce., sugar.
4. Place in a saucepan, and bring to a boil for 1 minute. Remove from the heat and let cool.
5. Marinate the beef in the refrigerator for at least one hour.
6. Put the skewers over hot coals,

# Cambodian Marinated Beef with Kime Sauce.

1 tbsp. Sugar
2 tbsp. lime juice
1 1/2 tsp black pepper
1 tsp. Water
2 tbsp. Mushroom soy sauce
2 tbsp. Oil
7 Garlic cloves (crushed)
1 romaine leaf lettuce
1 1/2 Pound Sirloin—(1/2 in cubes)

1. Combine sugar, 1 tsp. of the black pepper, soy sauce and garlic. Stir well and add the beef. Coat beef and marinade for 1-2 hours.
2. Combine remaining pepper with lime juice and water. Place in a small serving bowl.
3. Sauté beef in hot wok with cold oil, three to four minutes until medium rare. Arrange on platter on top of lettuce and serve with lime mixture.

# Mermaid Prawns

1 cup Red Curry
6 prawns—in the shell
2 tbsp. tomato paste
1 tbsp. peanuts. (chopped)
1 cup cooked spinach
12 fresh basil leaves
1 tbsp. chili paste
1 tsp. fresh ginger root (minced)

1. Shell and de-vein the prawns before placing them in from the sauce.
2. Combine the red curry paste , prawns, tomato paste, and peanuts. Bring to a boil, reduce the heat, and simmer about 5 to 7 minutes.
3. Cover the bottom of a heated plate with the spinach in an evenly.
4. Remove the prawns from the sauce and shell them. Arrange them on the spinach. Stir the basil and chili paste into the sauce and pour over the prawns. Sprinkle with fresh ginger and serve.

## Cambodian Sweet Soup

6-8 boiled eggs, (Shelled)
1 1/2-2 lbs pork, (cube)
fish sauce
soy sauce
pepper, salt
1-1 1/2 cups sugar
bamboo shoots. (sliced thin)

1.  Bring about 4-6 cups of water to a rapid boil. Add enough
    soy sauce to make a dark brown color. Add a couple dashes
    of pepper, dash of salt, sugar. Add 1 ¼ cup of fish sauce. Add
    about 5-7 tbsp. of soy sauce. Add pork and cook till near done.
2.  Add the boiled eggs to the soup, let boil for about 15 minutes,
    add Bamboo slices to soup and let boil on medium for about
    30 minutes.
3.  The eggs are taking up a shiny brown color. When eggs are a
    nice brown color, the soup is ready to serve.

# Cambodian Eggplant with Pork and Shrimp

1 Asian Eggplant
1 tbsp. Oil
4 Garlic (chopped)
1 to1 1/2 lb Finely ground pork
1 Fresh red chili, (minced)
1 tbsp. Soy sauce
1/2 tsp.p Fish sauce
1/2 tsp.p Mild chili powder
1 tbsp. Sugar
1/2 cup Chicken stock
1/2 c Water
2 tbsp. Spicy Lime Sauce
1/2 cup Raw shrimp, peeled and—chopped
Salt, pepper Garnishes:
fresh coriander
sliced green onions
2 Garlic cloves, peeled
1 Or 2 red chilies, stems (seeded)
1/2 cup Water
2 tbsp. Fish sauce
Juice of 1 medium lime
3 tbsp. Sugar
Shredded carrot, for garnish

Spicy Lime Sauce:

1. Combine garlic, chili peppers and the water in a blender or food processor and make a paste.
2. Combine fish sauce, lime juice, sugar and chili-garlic mixture in a small bowl.
3. Stir to dissolve sugar. If using sauce by itself, add a bit of shredded carrot for garnish. Makes 1 cup.

1. Preheat oven to 450 F. Puncture eggplant in a few places with a fork or skewer.

2. Bake on a sheet pan until soft, about 15 minutes. Set aside and let cool slightly, then peel and split lengthwise into strips about 1 inch thick.'
3. Heat oil in a wok or saucepan over medium heat. Add garlic and cook until lightly browned. Add pork, chili, soy sauce, fish sauce, chili powder and sugar; cook, stirring, until meat is cooked.
4. Add stock and water and bring to a boil. Add lime sauce, shrimp and eggplant; simmer until shrimp are done. Season with salt and pepper.
5. Transfer eggplant pieces to a serving dish and top with pork mixture. Garnish with coriander and green onions.

# Khao Poun Cambodian Spice Pork Ball Soap

1 cup cellophane (bean thread) or Rice noodles
6 cups chicken stock
1/2 cup smoked ham, finely chopped
1 small egg
1/2 cup pork, ground
4 oz water chestnuts, (minced)
1/2 tsp. cornstarch
1 tbsp. soy sauce

Garnish: 2 tbsp. green onions, minced

1.  Soak cellophane noodles in cold water for 15 minutes, then cut
    into 6-inch lengths
2.  Boil the stock in a large saucepan and stir in the soaked and
    cut cellophane noodles.
3.  Reduce heat and simmer till done.
4.  Meanwhile, mix together the minced ground pork, ham, egg
    and water chestnuts with the cornstarch and soy sauce.
5.  Shape the ground meat into little meatballs and drop into the
    soup. Continue cooking over moderate heat for another 10-15
    minutes. When ready to serve, ladle into bowls and garnish
    with scallions.

# Black Tiger Shrimp with Vegetables

1 lb. black tiger shrimp, shelled and de-veined (can substitute thinly sliced chicken breast)
1/2 cup lemongrass (minced)
1/2 cup cilantro (minced )
1 tsp. galangal (chopped)
1 tsp. coriander seeds
8 cloves of garlic
1. kaffir lime leaves
1 cup. tamarind pulp or juice
1 red pepper, cut into 1 inch diagonal slices (red bell peppers are an adequate substitute)
6 oz asparagus cut into 1 1/2 inch lengths
6 oz Napa cabbage cut into 1 inch diagonal slices
3 tbsp. vegetable oil
1 tsp. salt
1 tbsp. sugar
3/4 cup water
1 cup chicken stock

1.  In a blender: cilantro, galangal, lemongrass, coriander seeds, garlic, kaffir lime leaves and water. Blend into a very smooth paste and set aside.
2.  Soak the tamarind pulp in about 4 tbsp. of hot water for 5 minutes. Using a spoon, scrape the flesh away from the pulp to release the tamarind flavor into the water. Discard the pulp. Set the tamarind juice aside. Tamarind juice availed in Asian or Hispanic markets makes this easier.
3.  In a wok or a 12-inch sauté pan over high heat add 2 tbsp. of vegetable oil. Add the paste and stir constantly for approximately 2 minutes, until the aroma is released. Transfer the cooked paste into a bowl.

4.  Add the remaining tbsp. of oil to the wok. Add the shrimp and stir fry till pink and half cooked. Add all of the sliced vegetables and stir fry for 3 to for minutes, until the vegetables have reached your desired tenderness a. Add the paste, chicken stock, salt, sugar, and tamarind juice and stir fry for two more minutes.
5.  Garnish with cilantro leaves and served immediately.

# Khmer Coconut Pork

6-8 boiled eggs, (Shelled)
1 1/2-2 lbs pork, (cube)
fish sauce
soy sauce
pepper, salt
1-1 1/2 cups sugar
bamboo shoots. (sliced thin)

1.  Bring about 4-6 cups of water to a rapid boil. Add enough soy sauce to make a dark brown color. Add a couple dashes of pepper, dash of salt, sugar. Add 1 ¼ cup of fish sauce. Add about 5-7 tbsp. of soy sauce. Add pork and cook till near done.
2.  Add the boiled eggs to the soup, let boil for about 15 minutes, add Bamboo slices to soup and let boil on medium for about 30 minutes.
3.  The eggs are taking up a shiny brown color. When eggs are a nice brown color, the soup is ready to serve.

1 lb Pork (cubed)
1 stalk Lemon Grass, (thinly sliced)
1 large Onion, (chopped )
5 Garlic Cloves, (chopped )
1 tsp. The grated Zest of 1 Lime
1/2 tsp. Ground Turmeric
3fl.oz. Water
2oz freshly grated Coconut or unsweetened Desiccated Coconut
1 tbsp. Sugar
1/2 tsp. Salt

1. Place the lemon grass, shallots., garlic, lime zest, turmeric and water in a food processor and blend to a paste.
2. Transfer the lemon grass paste to a mixing bowl together with the coconut, sugar and salt and mix well.
3. Add the pork and mix to coat well. Cover with plastic wrap and leave to marinate for at least an hour at room temperature.
4. Preheat the grill. Thread the pork cubes onto skewers and cook for 10-15 minutes.

# Amok Trei Coconut Fish Curry Parcels

1 Garlic Clove, chopped
1 Red Onion, chopped
5cm/2-inches Galangal root, chopped or
1/2 tsp. Ground Galangal
2 stalks
½ tsp. Ground Turmeric
1 tsp. Paprika
2 tbsp. Fish Sauce
1 tbsp. Sugar
½ tsp salt
14 oz thin Coconut Milk
450g/1lb White Fish Fillets e.g.
4-8 Banana leaves (depending on size) or 8 large Dark Green Cabbage Leaves

1. Place the garlic, onion, galangal, lemon grass, turmeric, paprika, fish sauce and sugar in a blender or food processor and process until it is made into a paste.
2. Add the coconut milk and process again until thoroughly mixed.
3. Transfer the coconut mixture to a medium saucepan. On low heat bring to a simmer., stirring. Continue to cook gently for about 5-10 minutes or until thickened.
4. Meanwhile, if using cabbage, place them in a large saucepan, cover with boiling water and set aside to soften. If using banana leaves, cut into pieces about 20cm/8-inches square.
5. Place the fish in a bowl, season with a little salt then pour over half the hot coconut sauce and mix well. Set the remaining sauce aside.
6. Place 1/8th of the fish mixture in the centre of each leaf and fold the edges over to form secure parcels, making sure you tuck the edges under carefully.
7. In a bamboo or stainless steal steamer cook the parcels for 1 hour or till fish is done.

8. A few minutes before the end of the cooking, gently reheat the remaining sauce.
9. Make a small opening down the centre of each parcel and spoon the remaining coconut sauce into the opening.

# Khmer Star Fruit Steak

1 ½ lbs tenderloin steak slices
1 Ripped star fruit, seeded and sliced
3 Cloves garlic, (chopped)
1 tbsp. vegetable oil
1 tbsp. brown sugar
1 tbsp. soy sauce
1 tsp. sea salt
2 Hot chili
¼ tsp. black pepper
1 Cup water

1. Places steak slices in deep dish. Set it a side.
2. Put remaining ingredients. in a blender and integrate it well.
3. Pour sauce over steaks, covered dish and refrigerated it over night or at least 4 hours.
4. Cook steak over hot grill till desired doneness.

# Pork Brochettes with Shredded Coconut

16 bamboo wooden or metal skewers
(If using wooden skewers, soak them for
30 minutes in water to cover before threading meat.)
1/4 cup lemongrass paste
1/2 cup freshly grated coconut or packaged unsweetened shredded coconut
1 tbsp. sugar
1/2 tsp. salt
1 pound pork tenderloin, pork loin or fresh ham, cut into pieces.

For the Lemongrass Paste:

1 stalk lemongrass, thinly sliced
2 large shallots., coarsely chopped
5 garlic cloves, coarsely chopped
2 kaffir lime leaves, or grated peel of lime
1/2 tsp. turmeric
1/4 cup water

1. Blend all the Lemon paste ingredients. in a blender or food processor until smooth, approximately 2 to 3 minutes.
2. Combine the lemongrass paste in a bowl with the shredded coconut, sugar and salt, integrating well.
3. Add the pieces of pork and stir to coat thoroughly with the paste. Let marinate for at least an hour at room temperature or overnight in the refrigerator.

# Tamarind Chicken Wings

WINGS:
12 wings. Cut through joints
2 cups cooking oil.
½ tsp. salt.
¼ Cup All purpose flour.

SAUCE:
1 tbsp. cooking oil.
2 Cloves garlic. Minced.
1 Yellow onion. Chopped.
½ cup of Tamarind Juice
½ Cup water.
1 tbsp. cornstarch.
2 tbsp. fish sauce.
1 tbsp. soy sauce.
2 tbsp. sugar.
1 Hot chili pepper. Chopped. ( optional)

WINGS:
1. In a large bowl, marinated chicken wings with salt and flour. Mix well.
2. Heat up 2 cups cooking oil in a large frying pan. Normally about 350 F to 450 F
3. When oil hot , drops chicken wings in the fryer.
4. Deep fried wings till it golden brown.
5. Removed wings and place them on a plate covered with paper towel to drained off excessive oil.

SAUCE:
1. In a small bowl, mix water with cornstarch, fish sauce, soy sauce, sugar, tamarind juice. Mix well. Set a side.
2. Heat a small sauce pan with cooking oil. When it hot, sauté garlic, onion and hot pepper. Stir well. Add corn starch mix sauce and stir till sauce thicken.
3. Pour or bush tamarind sauce over fried chicken wings. Coat them well.

# Pakon Char Poat Koun

½ to 1 lb. Medium or large shrimp. Peeled and de-veined.
1 Dozen dried shiitake mushroom or
4-8 oz can of mushrooms
1 Large carrot (sliced thin)
2 Cloves garlic. (minced)
1 Yellow onion (Sliced).
4 Stalks green onion (sliced thin)
½ Cup All purpose flour.
2 tbsp. cooking oil.
2 tbsp. corn starch.
1 Cup water.
2 tbsp. soy sauce.
1 tbsp. oyster sauce.
½ tbsp. sugar.
¼ tsp. salt.
¼ tsp. black pepper.
A handful chopped cilantro for garnish.(optional)

1. In a large bowl, marinated shrimp with salt and black pepper, then add all purpose flour and cornstarch. Mix well and set a side.
2. In a small bowl, mix water with soy sauce, oyster sauce, and sugar. Set a side. Pre-heat a wok or skillet with high temperature. When it hot, add cooking oil. Sauté shrimp for few seconds then add garlic, yellow onion, carrot, baby corn and mushroom. Stir well. The prawns should almost be completely pink.
3. Pour mix sauces over and stir till the sauce thicken, then add green onion. Stirs well. Garnish with chopped cilantro before serve.

# Amok Fish

1 pound monkfish or cod fillets
1/4 cup coconut milk
1/4 tsp. turmeric
1/4 tsp. paprika
1/4 tsp. curry powder, optional
2 tsp. minced fresh ginger
2 cloves garlic (minced)
2 tbsp. thinly sliced fresh red chili pepper, seeds included
2 tsp. fish sauce
2 tbsp. oil
1/2 cup onion (sliced)
12 baby lettuce leaves
1 tbsp. shredded fresh kaffir lime leaves, if desired.
Salt and freshly ground black pepper

1. Cut fish into 1/2-inch chunks. Season to taste with salt and pepper; set aside.
2. In a medium or large bowl, combine coconut milk, turmeric, paprika, curry powder, ginger, garlic, chili pepper and fish sauce. Mix well. Add fish pieces, and toss until well coated. Let marinate 1-2 hours.
3. In a hot wok or skillet add oil and fry onions till translucent not brown), add fish fillets and cook till done.
4. Make lettuce cups in a bowl, and add fish. Top with Cilantro or kaffir lime leaves.

# TREY KHO MANOR CARAMELIZED
# FISH WITH PINEAPPLE

## Caramel Sauce (Tirk Kmao):

1 tabs sugar
1 tbsp water

heat and brown sugar and mix with water. Be careful, sugar burns badly.

Or Asian Carmel sauce from a jar.

# Kho

2 Cups water
1 (1-1 ½ lbs )Whole trout, or catfish,
cleaned and cut ½ inch thick
½ Pineapple, peeled and sliced
2 tbsp. fish sauce
1 tbsp. sugar
1 tsp. salt
2 Cloves garlic, minced
¼ tsp. black pepper
3 Stalks green onion, chopped

1.  Make caramel sauce first by put 1-tsp. sugar and 1-tbsp. water
    in a small saucepan. Cook on low heat and stir frequently till
    the sugar turns dark brown color, and not burn.
2.  Immediately pour 2 cups water to caramelized sugar. Add fish,
    pineapple, fish sauce, sugar, salt and garlic.
3.  Simmering till fish tender and water reduced.
4.  Top with black pepper and green onion.

NOTE: No doubt placing this on jasmine rice, or thinly sliced fried
potatoes goes recommended.

# Five Vegetable Stir-fry

2 tsp. vegetable oil
4 medium carrots (Sliced thin)
1 large onion—(diced)
1 large red bell pepper (sliced)
3 cups broccoli florets
3 cups red cabbage (sliced)
1/2 cup clear vegetable or chicken broth
3 tbsp. chopped fresh mint

1. Prepare Vegetables for cooking.
2. Heat 1 tsp. oil in heated skillet or Wok on medium-high heat.
3. Add carrots, onion, and bell pepper. Saute 6 minutes or till desired tenderness
4. Add 1 tsp. oil, broccoli and cabbage. Add broth; stir-fry until cabbage wilts and vegetables are crisp-tender.
5. Top with mint.

# Fragrant-Eggplant

1 large eggplant
4 tbsp. soy sauce
1 tbsp. cornstarch
3 tbsp. sugar
1/4 cup sherry
1 tsp. crushed dried red pepper
6 slices ginger,
4 scallions (chopped, separate white and green parts)

1. Remove stem end off eggplant. Dice eggplant into small cubes.
   Sprinkle eggplant with salt and place in a colander to drain. Let
   sit for 15 minutes. Squeeze as much liquid out as possible.
2. In a small bowl, combine soy sauce, sherry, and water.
3. Heat 2 tbsp. oil in a large skillet or wok. Add red peppers
   and stir. Add ginger, white part of scallion. Stir fry briefly
   until ginger becomes fragrant. Add the squeezed eggplant and
   sauté approximately 8-10 minutes, stirring occasionally, until
   eggplant is thoroughly cooked.
4. Add soy sauce mixture and cook over high heat until most of
   the liquid is reduced and eggplant is thoroughly coated with
   reduced sauce—about 5 minutes.
5. Combine 2 tbsp. water with cornstarch. And to pan and cook
   till thickens
6. Add chopped green part of scallions on top of each plate.

# Sweet and Sour Vegetables

1 20 oz. can pineapple chunks in juice
1 cup sliced carrots
4 cups chopped broccoli
1 onion, cut in wedges
1 cup water
1 bunch scallions, cut into 1 inch pieces
2 cloves garlic, crushed
1 tsp. grated fresh ginger
1 large green pepper, cut into 1 inch pieces

Sweet and Sour Sauce
1 cup unsweetened pineapple juice
1/4 cup cider vinegar
2 1/2 tbsp. soy sauce
1/3 cup brown sugar
2 tbsp. cornstarch

1.  Drain the pineapple, reserve the juice and set aside. Place the vegetables, except the broccoli, in a large pot or wok with 1/2 cup of the water and the garlic and ginger.
2.  Sauté for 5 minutes. Add the broccoli and the remaining 1/2 cup water. Stir, then cover and cook over low heat for 5 minutes.
3.  Combine the sauce ingredients. in a separate bowl. Stir in the pineapple chunks and the sauce mixture. Cook, stirring until thickened. Use low heat, do not burn.

*   One can use other sauces, meat, fish, poultry for the vegetables. Tofu or Tempe too.

# Cambodian Cucumber Salad

4 cucumbers (peeled)
1 tsp. salt
1 tsp. sugar
1 tbsp. rice wine vinegar
1 carrot (shredded)
4 tbsp. soy sauce
1 tbsp. sesame oil
Few drops chili sauce: Optional

1. Slice cucumbers lengthwise. Sprinkle salt on cut sides, then place cut-side down on paper towels to drain. And pat dry.
2. Slice cucumbers into 1/2 inch pieces. Place in a large bowl. In a small bowl, combine the remaining ingredients. Sprinkle on cucumbers and toss to coat. Let marinade an hour before serving.

# Hot & Sour Mushroom Soup

3 c Vegetable stock
1 tsp. Pepper sauce
1 stalk Lemon grass (finely chopped into rings )
3 Kaffir lime leaves
1 tsp. Sugar
2 tbsp. Lemon juice
2 oz Oyster mushrooms / or button mushrooms
2 red or green chilies

1.  In a large pan, bring the vegetable stock to the boil and stir in the Pepper sauce.
2.  Add the remaining ingredients. and simmer, stir well until the mushrooms are just cooked but still al dente. Pour into a serving bowl and garnish with Cilentro.

# Sweet & Sour Tofu Salad

2 tbsp. vegetable oil
1 garlic clove, crushed
/1lb tofu (cubed )
1 onion (sliced)
1 carrot (julienne)
1 stalk celery (sliced)
2 small red (bell) peppers, (seeded and sliced )
8 oz/ snow peas
/4oz broccoli
/4oz thin green beans, halved
2 tbsp. sweet soy sauce
7 oz Tamarind juice
1tbsp. soy sauce
1tbsp. tomato puree
1tbsp. light soy sauce
1tbsp. chili sauce
2tbsp. sugar
1tbsp. white vinegar
pinch of ground star anise
1tsp. cornstarch
1/2 cups water

1. Heat the vegetable oil in a large, skillet or wok until hot. Add the crushed garlic and cook for a few seconds.
2. Add the tofu and stir-fry over a low heat, until golden on all sides. Remove with a slotted spoon and keep warm.
3. Add the onion, carrot, celery, red pepper, snow peas, broccoli and green beans to the pan and stir-fry for about 2-3 minutes or until tender-crisp.
4. Add the oyster sauce, tamarind concentrate, fish sauce, tomato puree, soy sauce, chili sauce, sugar, vinegar and star anise, mixing well to blend. Stir-fry for a further 2 minutes.
5. Mix the corn flour with the water and add to the pan with the fried tofu. Stir-fry gently until the sauce boils and thickens.

## Tohu Char Kreoung. (Soy Gluten Rolls with Spicy Lemon Grass )

2 Large pieces Soy gluten roll. Rinsed under water and slices diagonally.
2 stalks of lemon grass. (Minced)
1 Small yellow onion. (Chopped)
2 Cloves garlic. (Minced.)
2 tbsp. cooking oil.
2 tbsp. soy sauce.
1 tbsp. sugar.
¼ tsp. black pepper.
3 Chopped hot chili pepper, or to your taste.(optional).

1. Pre-heat skillet, when it hot add cooking oil.
2. Sauté garlic, onion, lemon grass and hot chili pepper.
3. Add soy gluten rolls. Mix well.
   Seasoning with sugar, soy sauce and black pepper. Stir till coated.

# To Hu Ang Swai Chei (Grilled Tofu with Mango Slaw.)

2 Pieces firm tofu.
1 Large green mango. Peeled and shredded.
1 tsp. soy sauce.
Dash of black pepper.
¼ Cup vegetarian fish sauce.

1. Marinate tofu with soy sauce and sprinkle with black pepper.
2. Cook marinated tofu on hot grill till both sides golden brown.
3. Put shredded mango on a plate, places grilled tofu on top mango.

# Num Ta Leng Sap (Khmer Vegetarian Pancake)

BATTER:
1 Cup rice flour
2 tbsp. cornstarch.
1 Cup coconut milk.
1 ½ Cups water.
1 tsp. sugar.
¼ tsp. salt.
¼ tsp. turmeric powder.
2 Stalks green onion. (chopped)

FILLING:
1 Piece firm tofu. Mashed.
1 Cup dices jicima.
2 Cups bean sprouts.
¼ Cup peeled mung bean.
2 Cups water.
2 tbsp. mushroom sauce
2 tbsp. cooking oil.

1. Place mung beans and 2 cups water in a small pot. Cook till the beans tender. Pour the beans in colander to drain off water. Set them a side.
2. Mix rice flour, corn starch, water and coconut milk together.
3. Mix with sugar, salt, turmeric powder and green onion, mix well. Set a side.
4. Mash the tofu in another bowl with cooked mung bean. Add Jicima and mushroom sauce with tofu. Mix well.
5. Heat skillet, pour 1 tbsp. cooking oil when it hot. Sauté the tofu mixture in the pan for couple minutes then add bean sprouts. Stirs and remove from the heat and set a side.
6. Heat up a skillet with medium high temperature. When the frying pan is hot, Coast with oil.
7. Stir the batter again and pour a thin layer of batter in the hot frying pan. This will not work in a wok, use a crepe skillet
8. When pour the batter, spread it around the frying pan to form a circle, full moon shape. Spoon out some filling , and put in the middle of the crepe. Whne brown on one side, flip it over.

**Edit 3**

# Manor Kho To Hu (Caramelized Pineapple and Tofu)

Ingredients
1 lb fried tofu. (cubed)1 8 0z canned chunk pineapple.
2 tbsp. vegetarian oyster sauce (mushroom sauce).
½ Cup water.
1 Clove garlic. Minced.
1 tsp. sugar.
¼ tsp. salt.
¼ tsp. black pepper.
1 Stalk green onion. Chopped.
Fresh cilantro. Chopped.

1. If using canned chunk pineapple, drained and reserve juice.
2. Put pineapple, tofu, garlic, vegetarian oyster sauce and water in a small pot.
3. Add sugar, salt, black pepper, juice, and green onion. Mix well. Cook in medium heat till the water reduced. Top with cilantro.

*Eating method:*
Take a leif off lettuce, put a piece of pancake in with a slice of cucumber and a few mint leaves in side the lettuce. Wraps the lettuce and dips in sweet soy sauce

# To Hu Ang Swai Chei (Grilled Tofu with Mango Slaw.)

2 Pieces firm tofu.
1 Large green mango. Peeled and shredded.
1 tsp. soy sauce.
Dash of black pepper.
¼ Cup vegetarian fish sauce.

1. Marinate tofu with soy sauce and sprinkle with black pepper.
2. Cook marinated tofu on hot grill till both sides golden brown.
3. Put shredded mango on a plate, places grilled tofu on top mango.

# Salor Kor-Ko Sap. (Khmer Vegetarian Stew.)

1 Asian egg plant. (cubed).
1 Bitter melon. (removed seeds and cut chunks.)
2 Cups cubes fresh pumpkin (peeled and seeded and cut).
5 oz. Frozen chopped spinach or ½ lb. Fresh spinach. Chopped.
2 Slices fresh galangal root, or 2 tsp. Of galangal powder)
1 Kaffir lime leaves.
1 tbsp. minced lemon grass.
1 tbsp. mushroom sauce.
1 tbsp. sugar.
2 tbsp. roasted rice powder.
1 tsp. salt.
½ tsp. turmeric powder,
½ tsp. paprika.
1 Cup coconut milk.
2 Cups water.

1.  Place coconut milk, water, lemon grass, galangal, kaffir lime leaves, turmeric, paprika and garlic in a blender or food processor and blended it.
2.  Places eggplant and bitter melon in a soup pot. Pour the sauce over, and cover the pot with lid.
3.  Simmering for 10 minutes then add pumpkin and spinach. Cover and cook till the pumpkin tender.
4.  Seasoning with sugar, salt, mushroom sauce and roasted rice powder.

# Banana Blossom Salad (Nyoum Trayong Chaek)

1 banana blossom (1-1 1/2 pounds)
2 tbsp. fresh lemon juice
4 cups water
1 large whole chicken breast (about 3/4 pound)
1 cup mint leaves
1 cup basil leaves
1/2 pound mung beans sprouts.
1/2 small red bell pepper, thinly sliced
1/2 cup roasted peanuts., and coarsely ground

## Dressing For Salad (Tuk Trey):

1/4 cup water
1/2 cup sugar
1 garlic clove
1 small shallot
1/2 cup fish sauce
5 tsp fresh lime juice
2 tsp salt

1. Fill a large bowl with water mixed with the juice of 1 lemon. Set aside.
2. Remove the tough outer layer of the banana blossom and discard it, along with the undeveloped "baby" bananas inside.
3. Carefully pull away the next several layers of leaves, regularly cutting into the stem to make it easier to break them off (the aim is to keep the leaves whole if possible). Lay several leaves on top of one another and slice the leaves crosswise into 1/4-inch wide strips. To keep the leaved from turning black, place sliced leaves in the acidulated water, turning occasionally.

Continue in this fashion, releasing the leaves discarding the undeveloped bananas and cutting the leaves into strips, until you reach the "heart." Cut this center in half lengthwise, remove as many "babies" as possible, and slice the remaining leaves widthwise about 1/4-inch thick.

In a medium saucepan, bring the 4 cups of water to a boil. Add the chicken breastm return to a boil, reduce the heat and simmer for 10 to 15 minutes, until the meat is tender.

Remove the chicken from the pan and let cool slightly, then shred the meat with your fingers.

In a large salad bowl, toss all the vegetables, mint and basil together with the chicken. Setting aside a handful for garnish, mix in the ground peanuts. Add dressing and toss. Sprinkle with the remaining peanuts. and serve immediately.

Edit 5

# Cambodian Summer Rolls

Rolls:
6 cups water
36 unpeeled medium shrimp (about 1 pound)
4 ounces uncooked rice noodles
12 (8-inch) round sheets rice paper
1/4 cup hoisin sauce
3 cups shredded red leaf lettuce
1/4 cup thinly sliced fresh basil
1/4 cup thinly sliced fresh mint

Dipping sauce:
1/3 cup low-sodium soy sauce
1/4 cup water
2 tbsp. sugar
2 tbsp. chopped fresh cilantro
2 tbsp. fresh lime juice
1 tsp. minced peeled fresh ginger
1 tsp. chili paste with garlic (such as sambal oelek)
1 garlic clove, minced

1.  To prepare rolls, bring 6 cups water to a boil in a large saucepan. Add the shrimp to pan; cook 3 minutes or until done. Drain and rinse with cold water; drain. Peel shrimp; chill.
2.  Place noodles in a large bowl; cover with boiling water. Let stand for 8 minutes; drain. Add cold water to a large, shallow dish to a depth of 1 inch. Place 1 rice paper sheet in water. Let stand 2 minutes or until soft. Place rice paper sheet on a flat surface.

3. Spread 1 tsp. hoisin sauce in the center of sheet; top with 3 shrimp, 1/4 cup lettuce, about 2 1/2 tbsp. noodles, 1 tsp. basil, and 1 tsp. mint. Fold sides of sheet over filling, roll up jelly-roll fashion, and gently press seam to seal. Place roll, seam side down, on a serving platter; cover to keep from drying. Repeat procedure with remaining rice paper, hoisin sauce, shrimp, shredded lettuce, noodles, basil, and mint.
4. To prepare dipping sauce, combine soy sauce and remaining ingredients. in a small bowl; stir with a whisk.

**Edit 4**

# Bananas Cooked In Coconut Milk

8 large ripe bananas
2 cups thick coconut milk
2 tbsp. sugar

1. Peel and cut each banana into 3 or 4 pieces. Make coconut milk from the creamed coconut available in packets or tubs. Simmer coconut milk and sugar until thick and creamy. Add bananas and cook gently until bananas are soft but not mushy. Serve warm.

# Sticky Rice and Mango

1 1/4 cups rice (sweet or glutinous rice).
3/4 cup very thick coconut milk
1/4 cup sugar
3/4 cup very thick coconut milk for topping the rice (
1/8 tsp. salt
1/2 tbsp. salt for mixing with rice
1/4 tsp. rice flour
6 medium mangoes (peeled and sliced)

1.  Cook rice in a rice cooker till done. 2-1 ratio of water
2.  Heat, on low, 3/4 cup of coconut milk in a small saucepan.
    Add sugar and 1/2 tbsp. salt to the coconut milk and cook until
    dissolved.
3.  Remove from heat and pour into cooked rice. Stir to mix well
    and set aside to let stand for about 15 minutess.
4.  Topping Sauce: Heat the rest of coconut milk and add salt. Stir
    until the salt is dissolved.

**Edit 4**

# Baked Coconut Rice Pudding

90g3oz scant 1 cup short or sround-grain pudding rice
600ml/1 pint/2.5 cups coconut milk
300ml cups milk
1 large strip lime rind

60g/2oz cup caster sugar
stick of butter (40z)
pinch of ground star anise
fresh or stewed fruit

1.  Mix the rice with the coconut milk, milk, lime rind and sugar.
2.  Pour the rice mixture into a lightly-greased 1.4 oven dish and dot the surface with a little butter. Bake in the oven for about 30 minutes.
3.  Remove and discard the strip of lime. Stir the pudding well, add the pinch of ground star anise, if using, return to the oven and cook for a further 1-2 hours or until almost all the milk has been absorbed and a golden brown skin has baked on the top of the pudding. 4. Cover the top of the pudding with foil if it startsp.p to brown too much to wards the end of the cooking time. Serve the pudding warm or chilled with fresh or stewed fruit.

# Banana Rice Pudding

1 1/2 cups brown rice-cooked
1 cup nonfat milk
1 medium banana-cut in slices
1 can fruit (15-ounce can)—cut in slices
1/4 cup water
2 tbsp. honey
1 tsp. pure vanilla extract
1/2 tsp. ground cinnamon
1/2 tsp. ground nutmeg

1. In a medium saucepan, combine the banana and fruit slices, water, honey, vanilla, cinnamon and nutmeg.
2. Bring to a boil, reduce the heat, and simmer for 10 minutes, or until quite tender but not mushy.
3. Add the rice and milk and mix thoroughly. Bring to a boil and simmer 10 more minutes. Serve warm.

# Another Banana Dessert 2

3tbsp. shredded fresh coconut
60g/2oz cup unsalted butter
1tbsp. grated ginger root
grated zest of 1 orange
6 bananas
60g/2oz cup sugar
4tbsp. fresh lime juice
6tbsp. orange liqueur
3tsp. toasted sesame seed
lime slices

1.  Heat a frying pan on low heat until hot. Add the coconut and cook, stirring constantly, for about 1 minute until lightly colored. Remove from the pan and allow to cool.
2.  Heat the butter in a large frying pan until it melts. Add the ginger and orange zest and mix well.
3.  Peel and slice the bananas lengthwise. Place the bananas cut-side down in the butter mixture and cook for 1-2 minutes or until the sauce mixture startsp.p to become sticky. Turn to coat in the sauce.
4.  Remove the bananas from the pan and place on heated serving plates. Keep warm.
5.  Return the pan to the heat and add the orange liqueur, stirring well to blend. Ignite with a long match, allow the flames to die down, then pour over the bananas.
    Sprinkle with the coconut and sesame seeds and serve at once, decorated with slices of lime.

# Oranges in Syrup

4 oranges
8oz/225g sugar
12fl oz/375ml/1.5 cups water
1tsp./5ml rosewater

1.  Peel and separate the oranges, ensuring that no pits, pith or skin remain. Put the segments in a dish and set aside.
2.  In a small saucepan, bring the sugar and water gently to the boil, stirring occasionally. 3. Boil for 15 minutes, until it is the consistency of a thin syrup. Add the rosewater and blend by stirring. Pour the syrup over the orange segments and chill until required.

# Boua Loy

1 cup brown sugar,
1 egg, some
1 8 oz can coconut milk
bit of salt.
1 ½ cup rice flour
½ cup tapioca starch

1. Place rice flour and tapioca starch in a food processor or mixer. Add enough water and mix to make a fine dough.
2. Form little balls of about half an inch from the dough.
3. Boil some water and add the little dough balls. When they float up they are done.
4. In a pan simmer the brown sugar, coconut milk, and egg, mix with out poaching the egg.
5. Add rice balls. And coat them with the sauce.

# Filled Custard

-2 cups of finely shredded coconut
-1 cup of palm sugar
-1/2 cup of water
Ingredientsp.p for the wrapping:
-2 cup sticky rice flour
-1 cup of warm water
Ingredientsp.p for the topping:
-1 3/4 cups of coconut milk
-1/2 cup rice flour
-2 tsp.s of salt

Procedures:
1. The filling: mix the ingredients. and cook them until it looks right.
2. The wrapping: mix the flour with warm water. Use your hands to beat it until it is well blended. Make balls of 1/2 inch diameter before flattening it thin enough to wrap the filling ball.
3. The topping: Mix the ingredients. and heat it at medium temperature. Constantly stir it with spatula until it begins to set.
4. Put the wrapped ball in a small paper cake cup and top it with the topping.
5. Steam all these cups for about 10 minutes. Serve when it is a bit cooled off.

# Coconut Custard

8 oz/250ml/1 cup thick coconut milk
1tsp./5ml rosewater
80z/240g/1 cup sugar
0.5 tsp./2.5ml salt
3 eggs, lightly beaten (use whites only, if you have some to use up)

1.  Dissolve the sugar in the coconut milk, add the rosewater and salt and stir.
2.  Add the eggs (or beaten egg whites) and mix well.
3.  Pour the custard into a bowl or a scooped out pumpkin, squash shell, or young coconut. Put in the top of a bamboo or stainless steel steamer and cook for 30 minutes, or until set.

# Mung Bean Pudding

2 Cups pre cooked green mung bean.
Or mung bean flour.
1 Package 3.5 oz of dried tapioca pearls or shredded tapioca.
4 Cups water.
½ Cup palm sugar.
½ Cup sugar.
½ tsp. salt.
1 tsp. pure vanilla extract.

1.  Soaked dried tapioca pearls in hot water for 15 minutes. Drain and set a side.
2.  Place water in a soup pot, when the water boiled add cooked bean and tapioca pearls.
    Cook till tapioca is tender.
3.  Add palm sugar, sugar, salt, and vanilla extract.

# Num Tirk Doung

4 Eggs.
2 Cups all purpose flour.
½ Cup melted butter.
½ Cup coconut milk.
¼ Cup shredded coconut.
1½ Cup sugar.
2 tbsp. pure vanilla extract.
½ tsp. baking powder.
¼ tsp. salt.
Vanilla frosting
8 oz shredded coconut

1. Preheat oven at 325 degrees.
2. In a mixing bowl or food processor, creamed butter and sugar together. Add eggs. Mix well.
3. Add vanilla, baking powder, salt and coconut milk.
4. Blended in all purpose flour and shredded coconut.
5. Greased cake pan with cooking oil or butter.
6. Pour the cake batter in to the cake pan. Bake for 1 ½ hour or till cooked.
   Removed from the oven, wait till cake cool off before removing from cake pan.

# Bobor Trao Taro Root Pudding

2 Cups diced taro root.
1/3 Cup sweet jasmine rice.
¼ tsp. salt
2/3 Cup sugar.
5 Cups water.

1. Put taro root, sweet rice in pot. Pour water and let it cook in medium heat. Stir occasionally.
2. When the taro root cooked. Add salt, sugar.
3. Pour Coconut Dressing on top.

# Nom Kruob Kanau Sweet Mung Bean Rolls

This makes 30 to 40 Desert Rolls

1/2 cup dried split mung beans soaked overnight and drained*
Or mung bean flour
2 cups water
1/4 cup unsweetened coconut milk
1 cup 3 tbsp. of sugar
pinch of salt
5 large egg yolks

1.  Place the mung beans in a saucepan set over low-medium heat with 1/2 cup of the water and bring to a boil, stir occasionally.
2.  Reduce the heat to low, cover and simmer until all the liquid has been absorbed, about. Remove any bean skins from the pot.
3.  Increase the heat to medium-high. Add the coconut milk, 3 tbsp. of sugar and the salt and cook, stirring and scraping constantly, until the beans become thick and begin to pull away from the sides of the pan, 7 to 8 minutes. Remove from the heat and allow to cool slightly.

2.  Transfer the beans to a blender or food processor and process until smooth and thick ( if the mixture is too thin to be molded into rolls, return to pan and cook until sufficiently thickened.)

3.  Meanwhile, press the yolks through a fine sieve set over a bowl by rubbing them back and forth gently with a spoon—this can take several minutes. Set aside.

4.  Prepare the syrup by put the remaining 1 1/2 cups of water in a saucepan, bring to a boil and add the remaining 1 cup of sugar, dissolve by stirring. Return to a boil, reduce the heat to low and allow it to simmer without stirring until the mixture slightly thickens.

5. Once the mung bean paste is cool enough to handle, roll out small amountsp.p into little sausage shapes, about 1 1/2 inches long and 3/4 inches in diameter. In batches , dip the mung bean rolls into the prepared egg yolks to coat, then drop them into simmering syrup, without crowding , and cook for 2 minutes, turning once after about 1 minute. The egg coating will be opaque and shiny. Remove with a slotted spoon and serve warm or at room temperature.

# Tik Doung Coconut Dressing

1 large can 16 oz. Coconut milk.
½ tbsp. sugar.
1 tbsp. cornstarch.
¼ tsp. salt.

Mix all ingredients. in a small saucepan. Cook in low heat till sauce thickening.

# Fried Banana Nuggets

1 banana. mashed.
1 tsp. sugar.
¼ tsp. vanilla.
6 Sheetsp.p small size frozen spring roll wrappers.
( Cut the sheetsp.p into half. )
1 Cup of cooking oil.
1 tbsp. powder sugar.

1.  In a small bowl, mix banana with sugar and vanilla.
2.  Wrap banana in spring roll shell. Set a side when done.
3.  Heat oil in a small saucepan. When hot drop wrappings in and deep fry till golden brown.
4.  Remove from oil and drain on a paper towel. Sprinkle with powder sugar.

# Num Treap-Sticky Rice with Sesames

2 Cups un-cook jasmine sweet rice. Rinse
1 Cup water.
8 0z can coconut milk.
1 Cup of sugar.
½ tsp. salt.
2 tbsp. Vanilla extract.
½ Cup roasted sesame seeds

1. Cook sweet-rice with four-cup water. When sweet-rice cooked set a side. Pour coconut milk, sugar, salt, banana or vanilla extract in a large non-stick saucepan.
2. Cook and stir often till sauce thickening. Add sweet rice to the sauce and mix well.
3. Remove the sweet-rice from the stove. Spread the sweet-rice on cake pan and sprinkle. sesame seeds on top.
Use spatula to press the sesame seeds down. Cover and let the rice set for few hours, before cut in to square pieces.

# SAUCE RECIPES

## Camdodian Salad Dressing

1/4 c Lemon juice
1/4 tsp.p Chopped garlic
2 tb Fish sauce
3 tbsp. Ground roasted peanuts.
1/4 c Sugar
1/4 c Water-
Dash hot pepper
1 tbsp. Chopped coriander leaves
1-2 ea fresh red chilis-sliced
2-3 T chopped white onion

In a small sauce pan, cook sugar in water over med heat until it converts into a light syrup. Add the remaining ingredients., stir well. Let cool. Serve over salad.

## Basic Lemon Grass Curry Sauce

1/3 cup lemon grass-sliced
4 cloves garlic
1 tsp. galangal-dried
1 tsp. ground turmeric
1 Thai/ red chili-stemmed & seeded
3 shallots.
3 1/2 cups coconut milk
3 lime leaves
1 Pinch salt or shrimp paste

1.  In a blender or food processor puree the lemon grass, garlic, galangal, turmeric, red and shallots.
2.  Bring the coconut milk to a boil and add the pureed ingredients, lime leaves, and salt.
3.  Reduce the heat to low and simmer, stirring often, for about 25-30 minutes, or until lime leaves are tender and the sauce is a creamy constancy.
4.  Remove the leaves before serving.

# Red Curry Khmer

4 Thai/Red chilies peppers, dried stemmed & seeded
1 cup water
4 tbsp. paprika
2 tbsp. vegetable oil
4 cups Basic Lemon Grass Curry Sauce (above)

1. Break the peppers into small pieces. Pour boiling water over them to cover and let steep until they are soft,.
2. Combine the peppers, water, and the paprika, in a blender to make a paste.
3. Heat the oil in a wok or skillet, add the pepper paste, and stir-fry until it begins get darker in color.
3. Reduce the heat, to prevent burning. Stir enough of the paste into the Basic Lemon Grass Curry Sauce to give it a good red color. Bring to a boil, reduce the heat, and simmer for 5 minutes.

NOTE: If you do not want a hot and peppery curry, use an Italian sweet pepper. If you wish for mildly hot, add pepper flake to taste, or pepper oil (Available in Asian markets and Chinatown Market.

# Tirk khngay Ginger fish dipping sauce

¼ Cup fresh limejuice. (Approximate 2 lime)
¼ Cup hot water.
¼ Cup sugar.
¼ Cup fish sauce.
1/3 Cup fresh ginger. Grated.
2 Gloves fresh garlic. Minced. Option.
3 hot chili pepper. Chopped. (To your taste.) Option.
Directions

Mix all ingredients. together in a bowl. Stirs well and serve.

# Tirk sa-ieu chu p'em Sweet Soy Dipping Sauce

¼ Cup hot water.
1 tbsp. soy sauce.
1 ½ to 2 tbsp. sugar (or to your taste).
½ tsp. Sambal Olekek grounded chili paste. (Optional)
1 tbsp. fresh lime juice.
¼ Cup roasted unsalted peanut. Crushed.

Mix hot water, soy sauce, lime juice, sugar and hot pepper together.
Mix well.
Top with peanut before serve.

# Tirk Pahok-Pickle fish dipping sauce

1 Cup water.
3 tbsp. creamy fermented/pickle fish paste "pahok".
2 tbsp. minced fresh lemon grass.
2 tbsp. fresh lime juice.
1 tbsp. sugar.
1 tbsp. cooking oil.
1 tsp. grounded fresh chili paste.
2 Gloves garlic. Minced.
3 Chopped fresh hot chili.(Option).
¼ Cup crushed, roasted, unsalted peanut.(Option).

1.  Heat up a small saucepan in using high heat. When the saucepan is hot, pour cooking oil and immediately add garlic and lemon grass. Stir.
2.  Pour water into the saucepan, when the water boiled, stir "pahok" in.
3.  Remove from the stove before adding sugar, lemon juice and chili paste.
    Top with chopped chili and peanut before serving.

Taste the sauce the first time you make it. In the future, and increase or decrease "fish paste", or sugar to taste.

# Tirk trey chu p'em Sweet fish sauce

¼ Cup hot water
¼ Cup sugar
1/3 Cup fresh lime juice (approx 2 lime)
1/3 Cup fish sauce
3 Chopped hot chili pepper or to your taste (option)
1/3 Cup roasted peanut, crushed (option)

Directions
In a small bowl, mix hot water with sugar till sugar dissolved. Add lime juice, fish sauce and hot chili pepper together. Mix well and set a side to cool. Top with crushed roasted peanut before serve.

# Tirk umpel Tamarind sauce

1 Cup water
2 tbsp. seedless tamarind pulp
Or 4 oz Tamarind juice.
2 tbsp. sugar
2 tbsp. fish sauce
2 Cloves garlic, crushed(option)
2 Chopped hot pepper(option)

1. In a small saucepan, boil water and tamarind for 3 minutes. Stir.
2. Add sugar, fish sauce, garlic and hot chili pepper. Stirs till sugar dissolved.
3. Removed from heat, set aside to cool before serving.

# Tirk salouk swai Mango Dip

1 Ripe mango, peeled and diced
1 tbsp. fresh lime juice
¼ Cup chopped cilantro
1 scallion, sliced
½ tsp. salt
4 Chopped hot chili pepper or to your taste(option)

For chunky dip; mix all ingredients. together.
For creamy dip: put all ingredients. in food processor and blended
till well integrated.
This should take a few minutes ort less.

# Spicy hot pineapple sauce with peanut

1 tbsp. vegetable oil
1 Stalk green onion, minced
1 Cup chopped fresh pineapple or canned pineapple
½ Cup water
1 tbsp. kumquat juice(approx 2 kumquats)
½ cup lime juice
1 tbsp. sugar
½ tsp. salt
½ Cup unsalted roasted peanut
1 tsp. Sambal Oelek pepper paste or to your taste(optional)

1. Heat a small saucepan, add vegetable oil and saute' green onion.
2. Add pineapple, water, kumquat juice, sugar, and salt. Stirs and simmering till boiled.
   Removed from stove and set a side to cool.
3. Put peanut, pepper paste and pineapple sauce in a blender, blended well before serve.

# Tirk kreoung pahok Grilled fish with pickle

1 lb Fillet of catfish, basa or any white meat fish
3 Cloves garlic, minced
½ Cup fresh lemon grass , minced
3 Chopped hot Thai or Redi pepper (optional)
2 tbsp. vegetable oil
1 Cup water
1 tbsp. sugar
2 tbsp. fresh lime
2 tbsp lemon juice
½ Cup creamy pickle fish (pahok)
½ cup of chopped sweet basil leaves
½ Cup unsalted roasted peanut, crushed

1. Bakes fish at 350F. When fish cooked, meat is completely white put fish in a large bowl and break up fish meat.
2. Using mortal and pestles to pounded on garlic, lemon grass and hot chili pepper together, set a side.
3. Heat up a small saucepan, when it hot add oil, lemon grass mixture and fish. integrate well.
4. Add water, sugar, lime juice and creamy pickled fish. Stirs well. Simmering for 10 to 15 minutes then add sweet basil leaves. Stirs. Top with roasted peanut before serving.

# Tirk doung Coconut sauce

8 oz 1 large canned coconut milk
½ tbsp. sugar
1 tbsp. cornstarch
¼ tsp. salt

In a small saucepan, mix all ingredients. together and simmering
till sauce thicken.

# PAHAK:

1/3 Cup best fish sauce, 5 Cloves fresh garlic, sliced
2 tbsp. sugar
½ oz Fresh galangal root, sliced thin
1 lb Fresh medium size shrimp, rinsed under cold water and drained
12 whole hot chili pepper or Red Italian Pepper
10 days later:
2 cups shredded, fresh green papaya(or shredded green mango)
¼ Cup shredded pickled fish(Pahok)

1.  In a small sauce-pan add fish sauce with garlic, galanga and sugar together and cook till sauce bubbling.
2.  Removed sauce from hot stove and set a side to cool.
3.  In a large mixing bowl, mix shrimp and hot chili pepper together, pour prepared fish sauce over, intergrate well.
4.  Place shrimp and sauce in a glass jar press shrimp down in jar (tamping),
    Seal jar tight with lid and sun dried it for 10 days.
5.  After 10 days, pour pickle shrimp in a large mix bowl, add shredded fresh green papaya and fish sauce (nam, not nouc cham) mix well.
6.  Replace Pahok back to the jar and refrigerate for 1 to 2 weeks before serving.

NOTE Nam is a Fish sauce with pickled fish in a jar, not the fish sauce that is like bottled Soy Sauce.

# TIBET

# Beef Momos

Yield: 12-18 pieces

Dough
3 c All purpose flour
1 c Water

Meat Filling
1 lb Extra lean ground beef
1 Onion; chopped
1/2 lb Daikon, grated
spinach or cabbage,—chopped fine
1 Garlic clove; minced
1 tsp Fresh ginger; grated
2 ea Green onion; chopped (white—and green both; no roots)
2 tbsp. Fresh cilantro; chopped
Salt

1.  Mix flour and the water; knead and form into a ball. Let rise covered with a wet towel or plastic wrap for 30 min. Bring a large pot of water to the boil.
2.  Cut dough into 12-18 pieces and roll into small flat circles. Mash together all filling ingredients.
3.  Place a spoonful of filling on each dough circle, folding over and crimping to seal. Place momos in a steamer and steam on high for 30 min.
4.  Serve with a mild tomato salsa, made from chopped tomatoes, cilantro, green onions and garlic, soy sauce.

NOTE: You can use pastry discs from the supermarket.

# Lamb Momos

Dough
3 cups All-purpose flour
1 cups Hot water

Momos Filling
8 oz Lean ground lamb
1/2 Onion, finely chopped
1 c Chopped raw kale
1/2 c Cilantro, chopped
3 Cloves garlic, chopped
1 tbsp. Chopped fresh ginger
1 1/2 tsp Curry powder
1 tbsp. Sherry, vermouth or brandy
2 tsp Flour
2 tsp Soy sauce
1/2 tsp Cayenne pepper or 1/2 tsp.p Hot chili paste

Khote Filling
2 tbsp. Butter
1 Chopped onion
3 Cloves garlic, chopped
3 Jalapeno Peppers, Sliced
1 tsp.p Cumin 1
1/2 tsp.p Curry powder
1/2 tsp.p Dry ground ginger
1/2 tsp.p Tumeric
1 1/2 c Raw broccoli, chopped
1/2 Red bell pepper, chopped
1 1/2 c Mashed Baking Potatoes
1/4 c Chopped cilantro
2 tbsp. Yogurt
Juice of 1/2 lime
Salt and Cayenne to taste
1 Bunch Kale to line steamer

Dough:

1. Pour hot water over flour; mix with fork. When cool enough to handle, finish mixing with your hands until dough holds together. Wrap in plastic and refrigerate until chilled through.
2. Work one piece of dough at a time; pinch off a walnut-sized chunk, shape into a ball, knead several times, then roll flat on a floured board.
3. Place dough circle in the palm of your hand; in the middle of the dough, place about 1 tbsp. filling. Bring up edges and seal at top with little gathers. Leave a tiny hole at top for steam to escape during cooking.
4. Line steamer or bottom of skillet with kale leaves. Top with a layer of dumplings and steam over boiling water 15 to 20 minutes. If using a skillet use just enough water to cushion the Momos; replenish water as needed. Serve immediately, pairing Momos with soy sauce, ginger, and vinegar. May also be served with Achar.

Momos Filling: Combine all ingredients.

1. Melt butter in skillet. Add onion and garlic and cook over low heat until onion is limp. Add chilis and spices and cook a minute or two longer.
2. Add broccoli and red bell pepper. Cook until they are crisp-tender; then add mashed potatoes, cilantro, yogurt, lime, and salt and cayenne to taste.

# Shamday-Tibetan Curry

1 small Onion
3 cloves of Garlic
1 small piece of Ginger
1 tsp. of Salt
1 Tomato
2 large Potatoes
1 tsp. of ground turmeric
1 small packet of Bean Thread Noodles
Lamb or Beef
1 handful of Seaweed
Sesame Oil

1. Soak the bean thread noodles and the seaweed in cold water and leave for 10 minutes.
2. Peel the potatoes and cut into cubes. Dice the meat into cubes. Vegetarians can substitute tofu (bean curd) for meat. Finely chop the onion, garlic and ginger. Directions
3. Fry the onion, garlic and ginger in a deep sauce pan. Add the turmeric, salt and sesame oil. Stir well. Add the diced meat and potatoes. Stir well. Add 1 pint of cold water and 4.
4. Cook for 20 minutes (Gas mark 4). Once the meat and potatoes are cooked take the bean thread and cut into small pieces, rinse the seaweed, add to the curry. Cook for another 5 minutes. Lastly, season to taste and add the tomato. Serve hot with boiled rice.

# Tibetan Noodle Stew

2 cups cavatelli or other thin tube-shaped pasta
1 tbsp. canola oil
2 onions, thinly sliced (about 1 1/2 cups)
8 garlic cloves, thinly sliced
1 tbsp. minced fresh ginger
4 oz lean lamb, thinly sliced (optional)
2 tomatoes, cut into 1/4 inch dice
4 cups Chicken Stock or Vegetable Stock
3-4 tbsp. tamari or soy sauce
2 tsp. hot paprika,
4 cups stemmed, washed spinach leaves

1. Cook the cavatelli in 4 quarts of boiling water until al dente, about 8 minutes. Drain in a colander, rinse with cold water until cool, and drain again.
2. Heat oil in a wok or large saucepan, preferably nonstick. Add the onions, garlic, and ginger and cook over medium heat until nicely browned, about 5 minutes. Stir in the lamb, if using, and tomatoes and cook until the lamb loses its rawness, about 2 minutes.
3. Stir in the stock, tamari or soy sauce, and paprika and bring to a boil. Reduce the heat and simmer the stew until richly flavored and the lamb is tender, 5 to 10 minutes. Stir in the cavatelli and simmer for 2 minutes. Stir in the spinach leaves and cook until wilted, about 1 minute. Correct the seasoning, adding tamari or paprika to taste.

# Then Thuk—Noodle Soup

1 small Onion
3 cloves of Garlic
1 small piece of Ginger
1 tsp. of Salt
1 small piece of Spinach (frozen or fresh)
lamb or beef
1 table spoon of soy Source
2oz Plain Flour
1 table spoon of Oil

1. Knead the plain flour into a dough using only cold water. Cover and leave for a while.
2. Meanwhile, peel the , cut it in half and slice thinly. Wash fresh spinach leaves and chop into large chunks. If frozen spinach is used defrost thoroughly. The amount used depends on personal taste.
3. Chop the onion, garlic and ginger. Cut the meat into strips and slice thinly.
4. Fry the onion, garlic and ginger in a deep sauce pan. Add the meat and soya sauce. Stir well. Add two pints of cold water and the sliced mouli. While the water is boiling, take the dough and roll it thinly into a large chapatti-like shape. Cut the dough into long strips 2 inches wide.
5. Take the strips and tear them into small pieces. Throw the pieces straight into the boiling water. Cook for 5 minutes. Lastly, add the spinach and season to taste. Simmer for a few minutes. Serve hot.

# Sherpa Momos

Meat filling
4 chicken breast halves, meat removed and minced
2 minced onions
5 cloves garlic (or to taste), diced
1 large piece ginger to taste, diced
1-2 tablespoons soy sauce
salt, paper and accent to taste
1 teaspoon garam masala optional
a little oil or ghee (clarified butter) to moisten—mix these ingredients together well
Vegetable Filling Edit
3-4 cups vegetables, finely chopped and lightly steamed:
onion
cabbage
green beans
cauliflower
garlic to taste
ginger to taste
soy sauce to taste
salt to taste
1 teaspoon garam masala
optional: a little oil or ghee (clarified butter) to moisten
Dough Edit
3-4 cups flour
cold water
Directions Edit
Dough Edit
Mix flour and cold water to make a smooth dough
knead lightly and break off small pieces, rolling each into a thin round about 3 1/2 inches in diameter.
Meat filling Edit
Mix all ingredients together well
Vegetable Filling Edit
Finely chop and lightly steam or blanch the vegetables until slightly limp

227

season with minced garlic, ginger, soy sauce, salt and garam masala optional: a little oil or ghee (clarified butter) to moisten Momos Edit

Put a heaping teaspoon of the filling in the middle of each dough round.

Form the momo in any of the following traditional shapes, using one hand to pleat or pinch and the other to both hold the momo and keep the filling from oozing out:

Eight-pleated half moon shape;

Six-pleated round shape, with the pleats in the center like a top-knot;

The nine-pleated half moon shape with the ends brought around to almost touch; or the fluted half moon shape in which the ends have been brought around and pinched together to form a circle.

Arrange on a steamer coated with vegetable oil spray and steam, covered 10-15 minutes.

Serve with a dipping sauce. (I like soy sauce mixed with a little rice vinegar and sugar or chilli paste

# Sha-Balé-Meat Pastry

3 finely chopped medium Onions
1 tbsp. of freshly ground Ginger and Garlic
2 tbsp. of Cooking Oil
1/2 tsp. Ground Cumin
1 tbsp. of Cooking Salt
2 tbsp. of soy Sauce
1 tsp. of Sesame Oil
2 tbsp. of Hot Water
2lb Minced Lamb or Beef
6 cups of Self-Raising Flour
Cold Water

1.  Add the cold water to the flour a little at a time.
2.  Knead the dough for about 4-5 minutes.
3.  Leave the dough to stand for a while at room temperature.
4.  Add the hot water, chopped onion, oil, salt and spices to the mince and mix them well.
5.  Roll out the dough as thin as possible (on a well floured surface) and cut them into 4 inch rounds.
6.  Put 2 tsps of the meat mixture on the round and flatten it down a little.
7.  Put another round on top and pinch the edges together tightly.
8.  Deep fry the sha-balé in moderately hot oil (only cook a few at a time).
9.  Drain thoroughly on kitchen roll.
10. Sha-balé can also be shallow fried on a low gas (but remember to fry the mince and onions first).

# Kongpo Shaptak

1 pound top round beef
2 tbsp. oil
1 large red onion, chopped roughly
One half tsp. paprika
2 cloves garlic, chopped
I (1-inch) piece ginger,
chopped one quarter tsp. ground emmo (sichuan pepper, available
at large grocery stores)
1 tomato, chopped roughly
One and one half tbsp. churu (blue cheese), crumbled
1 cup water
2 jalapeno chilies, sliced thinly on diagonal

1. Cut the beef into thin slices about one eighth inch thick and
   one and one half to 2 inches square.
2. Heat the pan over high heat and add the oil. Fry the onion until
   brown with the paprika, garlic, ginger and emmo.
3. Add the beef and stir-fry until cooked through. Add the tomato
   and the cheese, and cook until the cheese melts.
4. Add the water and stir in the chilies, cooking for a few minutes
   more. Serve with bread or rice.

# Tibetan Spring Soup

1 chopped onion
1 tbsp. mixed chopped garlic and—ginger
1 lb diced beef
1 pt water
1 handful chopped Radish
1 c plain pastry chopped into—tiny pieces
1 handful lettuce
1 tbsp chopped coriander

1.  Fry the onion, garlic and ginger together for a minute and add the beef until it is sealed.
2.  Pour in the water and simmer for 5 minutes. Add the mooli and the small pastry pieces and cook a minute longer.
    At the end, drop in the lettuce and coriander and serve good and hot.

# Mar Jasha

(Butter Chicken)
Ingredients
Marinade
1 whole chicken cut up,
1 tbsp. tandoori masala,
1/2 tbsp. garam masala (cloves, cinnamon and cardamom powdered)
2 tbsp. lime juice,
1/2 tsp. cummin powder (jeera),
5 tbsp. of yoghurt,
salt
Curry
2 tomatoes puree in a blender,
2 onions chopped,
1 tbsp. ginger-garlic paste,
15 cashew nut paste,
1 1/2 tbsp. butter,
3 tbsp. cream,
1 tsp. chili powder,
oil

1.  chicken in the marinade for 1 whole hour. Heat oil in a non stick pan and fry the chicken for 10 minuts.
2.  ove the chicken and keep aside. In the remaining oil fry the chopped onions till golden , then add the ginger-garlic paste and fry sprinkling little water now and then till oil separates. Add the cashew paste, chili pd, tomato paste and cook for 10 mins. Add the butter and the cream and the chicken. Mix well and cook till done. Garnish with cilantro.

# Lamb Curry

1 cup plain yoghurt
1 tsp. paprika
1 tsp. curry powder
1 tbsp. soy sauce
1 tsp. each of ginger/garlic
1 lb boneless leg of lamb cubed
3 large onions coarsely chopped
1 tbsp. oil
4 inch piece of cinnamon stick
1 star anise
5 whole cloves
3 bay leaves
4 tomatoes
3 large potatoes quartered

1.  large bowl, combine yogurt, paprika, curry powder, soy, garlic and ginger. Add lamb, mixing to coat, marinate several hours (overnight if you want).
2.  a large saucepan, over medium high heat, sauté onions in oil several minutes until translucent. Add cinnamon, star anise, cloves and bayleaves.
3.  k several minutes until onions brown. Add lamb and marinade; bring to boil over high heat, then add tomatoes.
4.  Lower heat to medium. Cook, uncovered, 20 minutes. Reduce heat to low. Simmer, covered 40 minutes.
5.  Meanwhile, in a separate saucepan, boil potatoes until just cooked (10 to 15 minutes). Stir into the curry for the final 5 minutes of cooking to even out and combine the flavours. Remove the cloves, bay leaves, star anise and cinnamon. Makes 4 servings. If you wish you can accompany this with a pita or some rice as a side dish.

# The Dalai Lama's Momos

'This is the Dalai Lama's favorite I am told. Thanks to my Buddhist Monk friend for passing this on

For the Filling
1 pound potatoes
3 tbsp. olive oil
6 onions, chopped
12 ounces mushrooms, chopped
12 ounces grated cheese*
1 bunch fresh coriander, chopped
Pinch of paprika Salt and pepper, to taste *Consider substituting parmesan, asiago, or Sonoma dry jack for yak cheese
For the Dough
1 pound plain flour
1-3/4 to 2-1/3 cups water
For the Soup
2 tbsp. olive oil
1 onion, chopped
2 tomatoes, skinned and chopped
1 tbsp. chopped coriander
1 vegetable stock cube
1-3/4 cups boiling water

1.  To make the filling, boil and mash the potatoes. Leave to cool. Heat the olive oil in a saucepan and cook the onions for 5 minutes until soft. Add the mushrooms, cover, and cook for 5 minutes or until soft. Leave to cool.
2.  When all the vegetables are cooled, mix with the grated cheese, chopped coriander, salt, and pepper
3.  To make the dough, mix the flour with enough water to form a smooth dough.** Roll out, but not too thinly. Cut into rounds with a 2" pastry cutter.
4.  Taking each round, press the edges with your thumb and first two fingers, working around the circle.

5. On one side of the round, place a tbsp.ful of the cooled vegetable mixture, then fold over and press the edges together, making sure they are well sealed. Alternatively, hold the round in one hand, and with your thumb and forefinger gather the edges into a pleat at the top and seal.
6. Fill a small steamer with water, first boiling the rack so the dumplings do not stick.

* * * Bring the water to a boil. Place the momos on the steamer rack, spacing them well apart as they will expand and stick together if they are too close. Steam for 20 minutes, or until they are firm and glossy. To make the soup, heat the olive oil in a saucepan, add the onion, and cook till soft. Add the tomatoes and chopped coriander and cook for 5 minutes. Dissolve the stock cube in the boiling water and add to the pan. Bring to a boil and simmer for 15 minutes.

# Tibetan Noodle Stew

Serves 4

Ingredients

2 cups cavatelli or other thin tube-shaped pasta
1 tbsp. canola oil
2 onions, thinly sliced (about 1 1/2 cups)
8 garlic cloves, thinly sliced
1 tbsp. minced fresh ginger
2 tomatoes, cut into 1/4 inch dice
4 cups Chicken Stock or Vegetable Stock
3-4 tbsp. tamari or soy sauce
2 tsp. hot paprika, or to taste
4 cups stemmed, washed spinach leaves

Directions

1. Cook the cavatelli in 4 quartsp.p of boiling water until al dente, about 8 minutes. Drain in a colander, rinse with cold water until cool, and drain again.
2. Heat oil in a wok or large saucepan, preferably nonstick. Add the onions, garlic, and ginger and cook over medium heat until nicely browned, about 5 minutes. Stir in the tomatoes and cook for about 2 minutes.
3. Stir in the stock, tamari or soy sauce, and paprika and bring to a boil. Reduce the heat and simmer the stew until richly flavored and the lamb is tender, 5 to 10 minutes. Stir in the cavatelli and simmer for 2 minutes. Stir in the spinach leaves and cook until wilted, about 1 minute. Correct the seasoning, adding tamari or paprika to taste.

# TIBETAN PASTA

## Then Thuk-Noodle Soup

1 small Onion
3 cloves of Garlic
1 small piece of Ginger
1 tsp. of Salt
1 small piece of Mouli Spinach (frozen or fresh)
1 table spoon of soy Source
2oz Plain Flour
1 table spoon of Oil

Directions
1. Knead the plain flour into a dough using only cold water. Cover and leave for a while.
2. Meanwhile, peel the mouli, cut it in half and slice thinly. Wash fresh spinach leaves and chop into large chunks. If frozen spinach is used defrost thoroughly. The amount used depends on presonal taste.
3. Chop the onion, garlic and ginger. Cut the meat into strips and slice thinly.
4. Fry the onion, garlic and ginger in a deep sauce pan. Add the meat and soya sauce. Stir well.
5. Add two pintsp.p of cold water and the sliced mouli. While the water is boiling, take the dough and roll it thinly into a large chapati-like shape.
6. Cut the dough into long strips 2 inches wide. Take the strips and tear them into small pieces. Throw the pieces straight into the boiling water.
7. Cook for 5 minutes. Lastly, add the spinach and season to taste. Simmer for a few minutes. Serve hot.

# Tukpa: Tibetan Noodle Soup

1/4 C. butter
1 1/2 tbsp. fresh ginger root, minced
1 1/2 tbsp. fresh garlic, minced
1 c. red onion, diced
1 tsp. turmeric
1 tsp. curry powder
1 tsp. chili powder
1 tsp. Kopan masala
1 c. potato, parboiled and cubed
1 c. fresh tomatoes, chopped
4-5 c. water
1/4 lb. fresh flat egg noodles (I use 1 9-oz. plastic pkg. egg linguine)
1/2 c. fresh spinach, chopped
1-2 tbsp. soy sauce
1 tsp. salt
1/4 tsp. ground black pepper

1. Melt butter in a saucepan over medium heat.
2. Add ginger, garlic, and red onion. Stir-fry over medium to medium-high heat for 1 minute.
3. Add turmeric, curry powder, chili powder, and masala. Mix well and stir fry for 1/2 a minute.
4. Add potatoes and tomatoes. Stir-fry 1 more minute.
5. Add water and bring to a boil.
6. Add egg noodles and boil for 5 minutes. Stir occasionally.
7. Add spinach and boil for another 1-2 minutes. If soup is too thick, add more water.
8. Season with soy sauce. Salt and pepper to taste.

# Potato Soup

1/4 c Butter
1 tbsp. Minced ginger root
1 tbsp. Minced garlic
1 c Diced red onion
1/2 tsp Turmeric
1/2 tsp Chili powder
1/2 tsp Kopan Masala
3 c Mashed potato
4 c Water
1 c Diced tofu
1 c Spinach leaves, chopped
1 1/2 tsp White vinegar
1 tbsp. Soy sauce
2 tsp Salt
1/2 tsp Black pepper
2 tbsp. Chopped green onion
2 tbsp. Chopped cilantro

1. Melt butter in large saucepan over medium heat. Add ginger, garlic and onion and stir-fry over medium to medium-high heat for 1/2 to 1 minute.
2. Add turmeric, chili powder and masala. Stir-fry 1/2 minute longer. Add potato and mix. Cook and stir 3 minutes. Add water 1 cup at a time, stirring constantly with wire whisk to prevent lumps from forming.
3. Stir until mixture is smooth. Add tofu and spinach. Mix well and bring to boil. Add vinegar, soy sauce, salt and pepper.
4. Simmer 5 minutes. If soup is too thick, add water. Add green onions and cilantro and mix well. makes about 8 cups.

# Cold Cucumber Soup with Mint

1 hard-boiled large egg
1 tbsp. rice vinegar
1/2 cup chilled sour cream
1 Cucumber (peeled and seeded, and cut into 1/2-inch pieces)
1/4 cup fresh mint leaves (Chopped)
1/2 cup chilled well-shaken buttermilk

1.  In a bowl with a fork mash together yolk and vinegar to form a smooth paste and stir in sour cream until smooth.
2.  In a blender puree cucumber and mint with buttermilk and salt to taste until smooth.
3.  Add puree to sour cream mixture in a stream, whisking.

# Potato Curry

6 cups small potatoes (avoid baking [russet] potatoes as they don't hold up well)
1/2 tsp. fenugreek seed
2 tbsp. oil
1 large onion, coarsely chopped
3 tbsp. ginger, minced
4 cloves peeled garlic, minced
1 tsp. coriander
11/2 tsp cumin
2 tsp.curry powder
1 scant tsp. turmeric
2 tomatoes, coarsely chopped
1-2 dried hot peppers, left whole

1. Scald the potatoes in water until almost, but not quite, done. Drain thoroughly.
2. While the potatoes are cooking, sauté the fenugreek seed in the oil on medium heat until light brown, being careful not to burn them.
3. Add the onion and continue cooking for five minutes. Add the ginger and garlic and cook another five minutes.
4. Add the spices and saut briefly to release their flavors. Add the tomato, the dried whole peppers, and a little water. Simmer until the flavors meld together.
5. Cook on medium heat for about 30 minutes. Gently add the potatoes, stir, and reduce heat. Cook until potatoes are tender, adding water if the sauce gets too dry. If the sauce is too runny, simply crush one of the potatoes to thicken it.

# Tibetan Vegetable Soup

2 tbsp. ghee
1 tbsp. minced ginger
1 tbsp. minced garlic
1/2 c onion, diced
1/4 c white flour
4 c water
2 c mixed vegetables, chopped
1/2 c chopped tomatoes
1 c tofu, drained & diced
1/4 c green onions, chopped
1 tbsp. tamari sauce
1/4 tsp black pepper

1.  Melt ghee & stir-fry ginger, garlic & onion for 1 minute. Add flour & continue to stir fry for fro 3 to 5 minutes, till golden in color.
2.  Add water a little at a time, whisking constantly to keep it smooth. Add vegetables, tomatoes, tofu, green onions & bring to a boil.
3.  Add the remaining ingredients. Simmer for 10 minutes. Thin with extra water if too thick. Serve hot.

## Tibetan Vegetables

1 t Oil
4 oz Buckwheat
4 oz Onion, diced
8 oz Mushrooms, chopped
1/4 pt Red wine
1/4 pt Vegetable Stock
4 oz Walnuts
8 oz Spinach
1 t Rosemary
1 t Sage
Salt & pepper

1. Preheat oven to 375F. Heat oil in a skillet & fry the buckwheat for 2 to 3 minutes. Add onions & mushrooms & cook for a few more minutes.
2. Pour in the wine & stock & bring to a boil. Reduce heat & simmer for 20 minutes. Add more stock if necessary. Grind the walnuts finely.
3. Wash & cook spinach without water for 6 minutes. Drain off any excess liquid & chop thoroughly.
4. When buckwheat is cooked, remove pan from heat & let cool slightly. Stir in walnuts & spinach. Mix in the herbs & mix well. Season to taste.
5. Grease a 1 LB loaf tin & press in the mixture. Bake for 50 to 60 minutes till the top is dark brown & feels firm to the touch.

Let it stand for 10 minutes, than turn out onto a plate.

# Cheese soup Churu

This exotic mixture combines hot chili with pungent blue cheese, using a spice called emma that is similar to Szechuan pepper. Chop Beef by hand or in a food processor.

Ingredients
1/2 onion chopped
1/4 tsp. each of paprika, ground Szechuan or black pepper
1/4 tsp. each of minced garlic and ginger
1/4 lb beef (such as top sirloin) minced
1 jalapeno chili, seeded, finely chopped
1/4 tsp. vegetable oil
2 tbsp. blue cheese
1 tomato, diced
5 cups water
1/4 cup cornstarch mixed with 1/4 cup water

1. In large saucepan over medium-high heat, fry onion in oil until brown. Stir in paprika, pepper, garlic, and ginger. Add beef, stirring constantly.
2. When almost cooked, add chili.
3. Reduce to low, add cheese stirring until melted. Add tomato and water. Stir in cornstarch mixture.
4. Bring to a boil while stirring. Cook until mixture thickens slightly. Makes 4 servings.

# Tema String Beans with Potatoes

1 tbsp. oil
1/2 onion chopped
2 garlic cloves minced
1/2 tsp. paprika
1 inch pieces fresh gingerroot, peeled and finely chopped
2 large potatoes, peeled and finely chopped
1 jalapeno chili, seeded and coarsely chopped
1/2 tomato, chopped
1 lb green beans, cut diagonally in 1 1/2 inch strips
1/4 cup water
1 tsp. soy sauce
1/2 small red pepper, thinly sliced
Salt to taste

1. Wash and dry Bean sprouts thoroughly. Put on the rice wine vinegar and sesame oil. 2.
2. Add more if you want it more zingy. The rice wine and sesame oil add a smokey taste to the bean sprouts.
3. Cover and refridgerate until you're ready to serve. Before you serve add more rice wine and sesame oil.
4. A little salt but only before serving if you need it.
5. In large skillet, or wok heat oil over high heat. Add onion, garlic, paprika, and ginger. Saute 5 minutes or until onion is soft. Add potatoes, chili and tomato. Stir fry about 5 minutes until tomato is dry.
6. Add string beans and water. Simmer, covered, over a medium high heat 12 to 15 minutes or until beans and potatoes are just tender.
7. Stir in soy sauce, red pepper and salt. Makes 4 servings.

Note: If you wish when you are preparing the potatoes, cut them into strips about the same size as the beans.

# Corn Soup Ashom Tang

1/2 onion, chopped
1 tbsp. butter (or use oil if preferred)
1/4 tsp. paprika
1 clove garlic, finely chopped
1/2 inch fresh ginger, finely chopped
1 tomato, chopped
1 square (12 oz.) firm tofu
3 cobs fresh corn and 1 tbsp. cornstarch, or one 15-oz. can creamed corn and 1/2 cup frozen (or canned) whole kernel corn, drained
4 cups water
1 green onion, chopped

1. Sauté the onion in butter or oil in a soup pot until brown and soft.
   Add the paprika, garlic, and ginger and cook briefly.
2. Add the tomato and the tofu, cut into small cubes, along with the water.
3. If using fresh corn, cut it from the cob and add it to the pot, along with the cornstarch mixed in a little extra water. If using canned and/or frozen corn, add them both now.
4. Bring to a boil, and simmer for a minute, stirring to prevent sticking.
   Sprinkle chopped green onion on top each dish.

# Greens with Tofu

1 bunch Swiss chard
2 green onions, chopped
1/2 tsp. paprika
2 cloves garlic, chopped
1/2 inch fresh ginger, chopped
2 tbsp. soy sauce
4 blocks firm tofu (12 oz. each), cut into 1-inch cubes
1/4 cup green peas
1 tbsp. oil
1 clove garlic, chopped
1/4 tsp. ground black pepper

1.  Wash the Swiss chard and tear it into pieces, removing the stems.
    Heat a little oil in a frying pan, and stir-fry the green onions, along with the paprika, ginger, and 2 cloves of garlic.
2.  Stir in the soy sauce, tofu, and peas. In a separate frying pan, heat a tbsp. of oil very hot. Stir in the black pepper.
3.  Add the Swiss chard, still slightly wet, and toss to coat with the oil and pepper.
    Cover the pan and let it steam for 30 seconds.
4.  Spread the greens on a serving platter and pour the tofu mixture on top.

# Kopan Masala

1/3 c. coriander seeds
1/4 c. cumin seeds
10 black cardamom pods, peeled
15 pale green cardamom pods, peeled
25 cloves
2 cinnamon sticks, broken up
1 tsp. black peppercorns
1/4 tsp. fresh nutmeg, ground

Mix together and grind finely, but not to powder, with a coffee grinder, spice grinder, mortar and pestle, rolling pin, or food processor. Stir in an air-tight jar.

# Coriander Chili Sauce (Sonam Penzom Sibeh)

1 bunch cilantro
4-5 small green chilies or 2 jalapeño chilies
1/2 cup dried crushed red chilies
1 cup yogurt or 1 large tomato
4-5 cloves garlic
1 tsp. salt
1/2 cup water

Directions
Cut the cilantro into short lengths.
If you are using tomato, cut it into quarters.
Place all the ingredients. together in a blender and blend until just uniform but still a little chunky.

# DESSERT

## Cream Cheese Barfi (Sweetened Cream Cheese Cake)

1.5 lb cream cheese
1.5 lb sour cream
1 can sweet condensed milk
1/2 cup sugar
1/3 cup sifted flour
1/4 tsp. baking powder
1/4 tsp. salt
1/4 cup almonds, coarsely chopped
1/4 cup cashews, coarsely chopped
1/4 cup golden raisins
1/4 cup coconut, coarsely chopped

1.  a food processor, combine cream cheese, sour cream, condensed milk, sugar, flour, baking powder, and salt to a smooth paste-like mixture.
2.  r into a large bowl. To the cream cheese mixture, add almonds, cashews, raisins, and coconut; fold in thoroughly.
3.  ter a baking dish well and pour the mixture; smooth out the surface and bake at 325oF for 15 to 20 minutes, or until the top is lightly brown.
4.  Chill it overnight in refrigerator. To serve, cut into 2-in. cubes and top it with whipped cream.

# Sikarni

4 cups regular yogurt
2 cups sour cream
1/4 cup double cream
2 cups sugar
1/2 tsp. ground cinnamon
1 tsp. ground cardamom
1/4 tsp. ground nutmeg
1 tsp. saffron
1 cup unsalted, shelled pistachio nuts, cut into thin slices

1. In a large bowl, mix yogurt and sour cream together.
2. Pour the yogurt mixture into a large colander with a cheese cloth liner. Allow draining 3. for about 12 hours. Transfer the mixture into a mixing bowl. Dissolve saffron in luke warm cream.

A: the yogurt mixture add sugar, cinnamon, black pepper, cardamom, nutmeg, dissolved saffron, and pistachio nutsp.p; fold in thoroughly. Chill overnight in refrigerator.

B. Scoop a cup of chilled dessert into a serving plate, topped with a generous amount of unsalted, shelled, whole pistachio nuts.

# Rasbari Dessert (Cheese Balls in Cream Syrup)

4 cups ricotta cheese
2 cup cream cheese
1 can sweet condensed milk
2 cups sugar
1/2 cup flour, sifted
6 cups half-and-half milk
1 tsp. ground cardamom
1 1/2 tbsp. rose water
1 tsp. saffron
1/2 cup almonds, sliced into thin slivers

1. In a large bowl, combine ricotta cheese, cream cheese, flour, condensed milk, and 1 cup of sugar.
2. Mix thoroughly to a smooth, stiff mixture. Make 1-in. balls and line them up on the bottom of a well-buttered baking pan.
3. Bake in oven for 15-20 minutes at 325oF, or until the cheese balls are lightly browned. Transfer cooked cheese balls into a container.
4. In a sauce pan, pour milk; add cardamom and saffron. Allow slow simmer, constantly stirring, until the milk has thickened into a syrupy consistency.
5. Remove from heat. Pour cream syrup over the baked cheese balls. Add rose water and almonds slivers.
6. Refrigerate overnight. Serve cheese balls with chilled cream syrup.

# Khir (Himalayan Rice Pudding)

1 gallon whole milk
2 cups cream
1/2 cup butter
1 cup basmati rice
1 cup sugar
5-6 cardamom, finely chopped
1/4 cup coconut, coarsely shredded
1/4 cup golden raisins
1/2 cup cashews

1.  In a large cooking pan, heat butter over low heat. Add rice and stir for 2-3 minutes.
    Pour milk into the rice mixture.
2.  Add cream and sugar; stir thoroughly. Bring to a boil and allow to simmer over low heat, stirring constantly, for about 20 minutes, or until the rice has softened.
3.  Add cardamom, coconut, raisins, and cashews; stir well. Cook for another 10 minutes, or until the rice is cooked soft and the mixture has thickened to consistency of your like.
4.  Chill the pudding overnight in refrigerator. Serve with handful of toasted cashews.

# Carrot Barfi (Carrot Fudge Dessert)

2 cups carrots, finely grated
2 cups half-and-half milk
1/2 cup butter
1 cup sugar
1 tsp. ground cardamom
1/2 cup almonds, thinly slivered
1/2 cup golden raisins
1/2 cup cashew nutsp.p
A dash of red coloring

1. In a cooking pan, combine grated carrots and milk. Bring to a boil and simmer over low heat for an hour, until the carrot has softened.

2. Add butter, sugar, cardamom, almonds, raisins, and cashews; mix thoroughly.

3. Sprinkle a dash of red coloring and simmer the mixture, stirring continuously, for another 15-20 minutes until the carrot mixture has thickened.

4. Remove from heat and transfer to a well-butter container; spread into a 2-in. thick layer. Chill overnight in refrigerator. Cut into 2-in. cubes. Serve chilled, topped with sliced almonds.

# MONGOLIA

# MONGOLIA MEAT DISH RECIPES

## Mongolian Lamb

1 lb Boneless lamb (leg or shoulder)
3 tbsp. Soy Sauce;
1 tbsp. Cornstarch
2 Garlic cloves; pressed
2 1/2 tsp Cornstarch
1 tsp Sesame seed;
1/2 tsp Sugar
1 small pinch crushed red pepper
2 tbsp. Vegetable oil; divided
2 carrots; cut diagonally sliced thin
½ lb Scallions

1. Cut lamb across grain into thin slices. Combine 1 tbsp. each_
   soy sauce, cornstarch and garlic; stir in lamb. Add scallions,
   separating the white ends from the green. Add the white ends,
   and save the green. Let marinade 10 minutes.
2. Meanwhile, combine remaining soy sauce, 3/4 cup water and
   remaining ingredients. set aside.
3. Heat 1 tbsp. oil in hot wok or large skillet over high heat. Add
   lamb and stir-fry till almost cooked. Add soy sauce mixture;
   cook and stir until sauce boils and thickens.

# Mongolian Barbecue

3 lb Boneless Lamb Chops (sliced)
2 lg Green Peppers,
3 c Bok Choi, Shredded,
3 lg carrots. Shredded
2 lg Onions, Thinly Sliced
1/4 lb Bean Sprouts.
1 tbs Peanut Oil
Cooked White Rice
Chipatti, or
Pita Bread
SAUCE
1 1/2 c Dark Soy Sauce
6 c Water
10 Crushed Black Peppercorns
4 Star Anise
4 lg Cloves Garlic, Crushed
1 cup Rice Wine Or Sherry
1 tbsp. Sugar
2 slices greated Ginger
3 cups Scallions Or Leeks,
3 cups Cilantro,

1.  Simmer the soy sauce, water, peppercorns, anise and garlic for
    a few minutes in a saucepan, then strain and cool.
2.  Add the wine, sugar, ginger root, 2 cups of the scallions or
    leeks and 2 cups of the cilantro.
3.  Add the remaining scallions or leeks and parsley.
4.  Cook the meat on a grill, or wok. When it is cooked to degree
    of likeness, add to the plates and ladle sauce on top.

When eating, spoon on the meat to the chipatti or Pita bread. (or
any flat bread.

# Mongolian Beef

1 lb beef flank steak, sliced thin ly
4 cups peanut oil for deep frying
1 tbsp. light soy sauce
1 tbsp. dry sherry or rice wine
1/2 tsp. grated ginger
1 tbsp. peanut oil
2 cloves garlic, sliced thin
4 green onions, sliced Chinese style
1 tsp. hoisin sauce
1/4 tsp. ground white pepper

1. Marinate cut meat in marinade for at least 20-30 min. Drain marinade and separate meat into separate pieces.
2. In a wok or deep pan, heat deep frying oil to 375 F. Add meat all at once and stir fry.
3. Remove after 1 min. and allow meat to drain.
4. In hot wok add garlic and scallions and fry for just a moment. Add Hoisin sauce, add pepper and meat. Fry till coated and sauce it heated

# Mongolian Hot Pot

3 lb Boneless lean lamb
4 oz Bean thread noodles
1/2 lb Spinach
1/2 lb Bok Choi
1 qt Chicken stock
1 tsp chopped ginger
2 tbsp. chopped scallions
1 tsp Minced garlic
1 tbsp. Finely chopped cilantro

DIPPING SAUCE
2 tbsp. Sesame paste-=OR=-peanut butter
1 tbsp. Light soy sauce
1 tbsp. Rice wine or dry sherry
2 tsp Chili bean sauce
1 tbsp. Sugar
1 tbsp. Hot water

1.  Slice the lamb into very thin slices. Soak the noodles in warm
    water for till soft, then drain them and cut them into 5-inch
    lengths.
2.  If using fresh spinach, separate from stalks and wash well.
    Though frozen spinach is easier to use. Discard the stalks. Cut
    the bok choi into pieces.
3.  Combine all the ingredients. for the dipping sauce in a small
    bowl and integrate well.
4.  Bring the stock to a boil. Ladle the stock into the hot pot and
    put the ginger, scallions, garlic and coriander into the stock.
    This should be arranges in order so people can choose their
    ingredient.

This dish also works great with other foods such as steak, fish,
oysters, shrimp, squid, mushrooms and tofu, The Koreans and
Vietnamese have a similar thing. There are several good cooking
vessels for this.

The Koreans have a cooking device called Shinsolo, and The Vietnamese have a soup pot, the has a base so a flame can be placed under it. A wide sauce pan can n\be used.

This is a shared dish entertained buffet style, but you can arrange this recipe to be more individual.

# VIETNAM

# Vietnamese-Style Carrot and Daikon Pickles

1/2 pound daikon, peeled
1/2 pound large carrots, peeled
1 tsp kosher or sea salt
1 cup unseasoned rice vinegar
3 tbs palm sugar
1 tbs white or black sesame seeds
1 cup water.

1. Wash daikon and carrots and cut into matchstick sizes, or shred for coleslaw.
2. In bowl, mix vinegar, salt, sugar and water until the sugar dissolves.
3. Add the carrots and daikon to the mixture and let stand for at 1 hour, then mix in sesame seeds.

Note: there are good shredders available, though best results are with a food processor. Napa Cabbage could be substituted for Daikon. Or a 16 oz bag of good coleslaw mix.

# Rice Noodle Garnish

8 ounces rice vermicelli
2 handfuls bean sprouts
1 small cucumber. Sliced
1/2 mint
2 scallions, thinly sliced
¼ head of lettuce, chopped fine
1/4 cup chopped roasted peanuts,

1. Cook rice vermicelli according to package direction, broad noodles can be used also.
2. Take the remaining ingredients and integrate well. Add the cooled rice vermicelli.

Note: Alternative these can be used in the bread with meat. Or replace the noodle with tofu. Or mix and match recipes. Lime juice and fresh herbs, as mint, lemon basil Cilantro, and a variety of others can be used. Explore your local and Asian market.

# Bahn Mi

4 boneless pork loin chops,
2 stalks of lemmon grass
2 tbs Soy Sauce
2 Tbs fish sauce
Baguettes or Italian bread, split lengthwise
Mayonnaise
1 ounce chille sauce with garlic (optional)
1/4 cup fresh lime juice
1 small onion
1 medium cucumber
a few sprigs cilantro Chopped
salt and pepper

1. Marinate pork chops in lemon grass, soy sauce and fish sauce for 1 hour.
2. Preheat the broiler on normal or use a grill. Place the pork chops on a broiling pan and set under the broiler. Cook browned on each side.
3. Open the bead loaves and spread mayonnaise on the insides. Place one of the cooked pork chops into each roll.
4. Spread chile sauce on the meat. Sprinkle with a little lime juice and top with slices of onion, cucumber, cilantro, salt and pepper.

Note: there is no measurement for mayonnaise, spread it on with a butter knife. As far as Baguettes and bread goes, some recipes say 6 inch baguette or seven. In the supermarket, I see no measurements for them, maybe 7 inches. There are bigger loaves and varied types of bread that can be used, even Portuguese rolls.

I usually buy 4 small baguettes or cut the large loaf in half.

# Mahi Mahi Banh Mi

baguettes
1 tbs unsalted sweet butter, melted
2 tablespoons mayonnaise
2 scallions, sliced lengthwise and cut into 2-inch pieces
1/2 carrot, shredded or julienned
1/2 cucumber, julienned
1 lb Mahi Mahi fillets (or salmon, whiting, or Pollock)
1/2 bunch fresh cilantro and/or mint, chopped
1/2 bunch watercress, hard stems removed

Asian chili sauce

60 ml (¼ cup) fish sauce
60 ml (¼ cup) rice vinegar
2 tbsp white sugar
125ml (½ cup) water
2 garlic cloves, finely chopped
1 red chili, finely chopped
2 tbsp lime juice

1. Preheat the broiler or grill. Split the baguette or rolls. Broil until lightly toasted, about 2 minutes. Butter the rolls.
2. Remove from the broiler and spread both sides with mayonnaise. Toss the scallions, carrot and cucumber in the dressing. Stack the sandwiches with Mahi Mahi, Add sauce.

Note: keep in mind when cooking small slices of pork, they may not brown, but turn white. Also, I recommend a electric or stove top grill. Don't forget to oil them. For varied marinades add lemon grass to meat. Slice the stalks thin.

# Banh mi With Mushu Pancake

1/2 cup sugar
1/2 cup distilled white vinegar
1/2 tsp kosher salt
4 cups shredded carrots
1/4 cup soy sauce
2 tablespoons fish sauce
2 teaspoons sugar
1 teaspoon five-spice powder
1 teaspoon Curry (garam masala)
1/2 teaspoon freshly ground black pepper
2 cloves garlic, crushed
1 small shallot, minced
1 lb (1/2-1/4 inch thick) boneless center-cut pork loin chops
4 oz pickles carrots
4 flour tortillas or Mushu Pancakes
Mayonnaise
1 cucumber, sliced thinly
½ cup cilantro
1//2 cup fresh mint
½ cup Lemon Basil
4 Chilies
2 limes, each cut into 4 wedges

1. Place pickled carrots: In a large bowl, whisk together the sugar, vinegar, and salt until dissolved. Add the carrots, toss to coat and allow to marinate for about 2 hours.
2. Marinate pork in soy sauce, fish sauce, sugar, five-spice powder, garam masala, black pepper, and garlic 1 hour.
3. In a wok or skillet. add oil and place in pork chops

4. Turn chops until cooked; it should be a caramel brown color on each side.
5. Pace pork on bread with pickled carrots on bread.

* Note when broiling pork chops add water to bottom of pan. Best yet, get a stove top or electric grill to make them. Do not over cook as they will dry out.

# Grilled Meatballs

2 large garlic cloves, minced
2 Thai chilies
1 large shallot, thinly sliced
3 tablespoons rice wine or dry white wine
16 oz-ounce can plain tomato sauce
3 1/2 tablespoons Asian fish sauce
1 1/2 pounds ground pork
1/2 cup minced onion
1 cup water chestnuts, minced
3 tablespoons cornstarch
¼ cup chopped cilantro leaves,
1 tablespoon Asian pickled cabbage or Kimchi
2 teaspoons soy sauce
1 1/2 teaspoons freshly ground pepper
1/2 teaspoon sesame oil
1 large egg beaten with 2 tablespoons water
7-inch baguette or Italian bread
Pickled Carrots

1.  In a skillet or wok, heat 2 tablespoons of the oil. Add the garlic, chiles and shallot and cook over moderate heat until softened, about 3 minutes. Add the rice wine and bring to a boil. Then Stir in the tomato sauce and simmer, stirring occasionally, until. Stir in 1 tablespoon of the fish sauce.
2.  In a large bowl mix the ground pork with the onion, water chestnuts, cornstarch, chopped cilantro, Asian pickled cabbage, soy sauce, pepper, sesame oil, beaten egg mixture and 2 1/2 tablespoons of fish sauce.
3.  Roll the mixture into small meatballs. Thread the meatballs onto the skewers. It is preferred to use stainless steel over bamboo skewers.

4. On a grill. Lightly brush the meatballs with vegetable oil and grill and cook till browned.

5. Split the rolls s lengthwise without cutting all the way through. Halve the meatballs, place them into the rolls and spoon the tomato sauce over them. Top with the Pickled Carrots and cilantro.

# Viet Steak Sandwich

3 tbs fish sauce
3 tbs limejuice
4 teaspoons brown sugar
1/2 teaspoon white pepper
1 lb flank steak, thinly sliced
1 tsp cooking oil
2 large tbs mayonnaise
4 small baguettes,
2 small carrots, shredded
½ small cucumber, sliced
1/2 cup shredded peeled daikon radish
3 scallions, thinly sliced
1/3 cup cilantro, chopped

1. Blend fish sauce, lime juice, brown sugar and pepper in a bowl until the sugar dissolves. Set aside 2 tablespoons of the sauce in a small bowl.
2. Marinate the steak with in the above ingredients for one hour. Grill steaks till cooked.
3. Blend mayonnaise to the reserved sauce. Spread the mixture on baguettes, top with the marinated steak, carrots, cucumber, daikon, scallions and cilantro. Slice the sandwiches in half.

# Viet Chicken Sandwhich

Mayonnaise
1/3 cup finely chopped fresh cilantro
3 tablespoons finely chopped red or green pepper
3 tablespoons rice wine or white wine vinegar
16 oz pickled Carrot
1 small onion, halved and thinly sliced
1/2 cup chicken broth
2 tablespoons hoisin sauce
1 lb chicken meat shredded
4 Baguette or Italian rolls

1. Mix Mayonnaise, cilantro pepper and vinegar in blender or food processor until smooth. Season, if desired, with salt and pepper. Reserve 1/4 cup mayonnaise mixture; refrigerate.
2. Combine remaining mayonnaise mixture, pickled carrots mix and onion in medium bowl. Season with salt and pepper. Let it stand 15 minutes.*
3. Bring broth and hoisin sauce to a boil in 12-inch skillet over high heat. Reduce heat to low, then stir in chicken. Simmer, stirring occasionally, 5 minutes or until heated through.
   Evenly spread rolls with reserved mayonnaise. Top with turkey and pickled carrots.

Note: You probably already guessed that you can substitute any, meat, cjicken, turkey. Beef or pork.

# Grilled Pork Paboy

2 scallions, minced
1 fresh red or green chile pepper seeded and minced
2 cloves garlic, minced
4 tbs sugar,
1/4 teaspoon ground black pepper
2 tablespoons Vietnamese fish sauce
1 1/2 tablespoons lime juice
1 ½ lb pork tenderloin,
1 cup rice wine vinegar
1/4 teaspoon crushed red pepper
1/4 teaspoon salt
large baguttes or italian bread
2 carrots, peeled and thinly sliced
1 cup thinly sliced daikon
2 teaspoons vegetable oil
Mayonnaise
1/2 cucumber, peeled and thinly sliced
3 Asian or serrano peppers, seeded and thinly sliced
Fresh cilantro leaves

1. Marinate pork with scallions, minced chile pepper, garlic, 1 tablespoon of the sugar, black pepper, fish sauce, and lime juice and stir until sugar is dissolved. Coat the pork, evenly, let it marinate over night
2. In a small saucepan combine the vinegar, remaining 3 tablespoons of sugar, crushed red pepper, and salt and bring to a boil, stirring until sugar and salt are dissolved. Remove from the heat and cool slightly.
3. Slice the bread length wise and toast On a grill or wok, add oil and cook the pork chops till done.

4. Spread mayonnaise on toast than place the pork chop slices in on.
5. Top with cucumber slices, pickled carrot and daikon mixture, and sliced peppers to taste. Garnish with cilantro leaves then place the top of the sandwich over all. Cut each sandwich in half.

# Grilled Pork

1 pound boneless pork shoulder steak,
11/2 to 2 tablespoons granulated or light brown sugar
1 tablespoon chopped garlic
1 tablespoon chopped shallot or onion
1 stalk lemongrass finely chopped
black pepper
1 1/2 teaspoon dark soy sauce
1 1/2 tablespoon fish sauce
1 tablespoon oil

1.  Cut the pork shoulder steak into pieces about 3 to 4 inches or
    you may shred.
2.  Place the sugar, garlic, shallot and lemongrass into an
    food processor or blender and process to a fine texture. As
    an alternative, mince the garlic, shallot, and lemongrass
    individually, put them into a bowl, and add the sugar.) Add
    the pepper, soy sauce, fish sauce, and oil and process to mix
    well.
3.  Add the pork, and coat well. Cover and set aside to marinate
    for 1 hour. Or, refrigerate up to 1 to 2 hours.
4.  Preheat a grill to medium-high, coat with oil. Grill for turning
    frequently, until cooked through.

Note: No doubt anyone can make a sandwich. Adding any grilled
meat, lunch meats like smoked turkey, lettuce and tomato. If you
have any left over meat from an Asian meal, add it to a baguette
or bread of choice. Throw on some bean sprouts. Peanut dressing?
Soy Ginger dressing. Use your imagination.

# Char Siu Pork

1 ½ lb pork chops
2 to 3 teaspoons kecap manis,
1 tsp Chinese 5-spice powder

1. Heat a skillet or wok add oil. Add the pork cook til almost done
2. add the kecap manis and sprinkle a little the Chinese 5-spice powder.
3. Make sure the pork is coated similar to a glaze.

# Kecap Manis

1/4 to 1/2 Soy Sauce
1/4 to 1/2 cup palm Sugar or molasses

1. In small pot, add brown sugar and soy sauce. Boil the sauce over low to medium heat until thickens Do not over boil, just cook till thickens than turn off heat and remove.

# Thai Iced Tea

Ingredients
4 cups water
6 black tea bags
1 tsp annatto
4 whole cardamom
2 tsp Annatto
1 can sweetened condensed milk

1. Bring water to a boil in a medium saucepan. Reduce heat and place all ingredients into the pan to infuse for about 10 minutes.
2. Remove from heat and let cool. Fill glass with ice and pour tea about 2/3 full then pour sweetened condensed milk to fill the glass. Mix well.

# Vietname Bubble Drinks

The origin is Chun Shui Tang teahouse in Taichung, where Ms. Lin Hsiu Hui (product development manager) poured sweetened tapioca balls into the tea during a meeting in 1988. The beverage was well received by the people at the meeting, leading to its inclusion on the menu, ultimately becoming the franchise's top-selling product.[2] An alternative origin is the Hanlin teahouse in Tainan, Taiwan, owned by Tu Tsong-he. He made tea using traditional white tapioca, which has the appearance of pearls, supposedly resulting in the so-called "pearl tea". Shortly after, Hanlin changed the white tapioca balls to the black version that is seen most today. The drink became popular in most parts of East and Southeast Asiaduring the 1990s.

Different flavorings can be added to bubble tea. Some widely available fruit flavors include strawberry, green apple, passion fruit, mango, lemon, watermelon, grape, lychee, peach, pineapple, cantaloupe, honeydew, banana, avocado, coconut, kiwi, and jackfruit. Other popular non-fruit flavors include taro, pudding, chocolate, coffee, mocha, barley, sesame, almond, ginger, lavender, rose, caramel and violet. Some of the sour fruit flavors are available in bubble tea without milk only as the acidity tends to curdle the milk. Maybe Coconut milk or soy milk could be a good substitute. I make mine with:

1. 1 can Sweetened condensed milk
2. 8 oz Tropical Juice or tea
3. 8 oz Ice

Place in a blender and then add tapioca balls.

6 cups cold water
1 cup tapioca pearls
1/2 cup <u>Sugar Syrup</u>

1. Boil water in stock pot. Add the tapioca; return to a boil. Reduce heat, cover, and boil gently 30 minutes.
2. Remove from heat. Let tapioca sit 25 minutes in water, covered.
3. Drain and rinse in a colander under cool running water. Pour Sugar Syrup over tapioca; use within 4 to 5 hours or refrigerate

Note: If you wish, do away with the condensed milk and use soy milk, or almond milk or a health food product.

Many South East Asian recipes are relative. The tropical climate in many places lead to common food ingredients, so some Indonesian dishes may resemble Vietnamese dishes and so on.

A Vietnamese cookbook is being considered, but there is many published. One thing that seems to be and issue is that there are many Vietnamese cookbooks and I would need to find something unique to add. I chose Vietnamese sandwiches because they would not be redundant and there are Vietnamese sandwich shops opening everywhere.

I discovered Vietnamese sandwiches in New York City. In Chinatown there where street venders offering Vietnamese treats. And among t hem where these.

The French certainly have left their mark on Vietnam with Coffee and other items. of course the Vietnamese did not invent or use mayonnaise much.

In the Vietnamese language these sandwiches would be referred to as e.g. bánh mì xíu mại for a baguette with crushed pork meatball, Bánh mì pâté chả thịt for a baguette or sandwich with pâté, Vietnamese sausage and meat, usually pork bellies, since it is the most common kind of meat. Almost all of these varieties innovations made by or introduced and is often eaten in Saigon and is known as bánh mì Sài Gòn ("Saigon-Style" banh mi), the most popular form is banh mi thit ("thit" means "meat") However, even in Vietnam, "a bánh mì for breakfast" implies a meat-filled sandwich for breakfast, not just bread. Which means Wraps, as Mu Shu Pancakes are included.

The Vietnamese sandwich, sometimes called a "bánh mì" sandwich, or a pho sandwich at times, is a product of French colonialism inIndochina, combining ingredients from the French (baguettes, pâté and mayonnaise) with native Vietnamese ingredients, such ascilantro, fish sauce, and pickled carrots.

The classic version, bánh mì thịt nguội, sometimes known as bánh mì đặc biệt or "special combo", is made with various Vietnamese cold cuts, such as sliced pork or pork bellies, chả lụa, and head cheese, along with the liver pâté and vegetables.

Some restaurants also offer bánh mì chay, a vegetarian option, made with tofu or seitan. In Vietnam, vegetarian sandwiches are rarely found on the streets. They are usually made at Buddhist temples during special religious events.

Another option is the breakfast bánh mì, either with scrambled eggs served in a baguette; the version eaten more widely for breakfast in Vietnam is eggs fried sunny-side-up with onions, sprinkled with soy sauce or Maggi sauce, and eaten with a fresh (and sometimes buttered) baguette.

One of the best Sandwich shops around Can be found in Philadelphia's Chinatown.

QT Sandwich shop 48 S 10 th Street, Philadelphia, PA. Just down from the bus station.

They have great sandwiches and Bubble drinks.

I have eaten in many Vietnamese places, and enjoy the Pho, the

BBQ with Lemon Grass, and more. Saigon Vietnam Sandwich Deli in New York is on 369 Broome Street. Sounds like a place on can really sweep up, so these are great places for sandwiches.

The shop is between Mott and Elizabeth Street.

In Chinatown, there are many Vegetarian Restaurants that use Seiten as "Vegetarian Meat". This product is a artificial meat made from wheat. I had Seiten Shrimp and it looks and tastes like real shrimp. This great for people who crave meat yet are vegetarians. This is an incredible invention for and one who swears off meat in exchange for a Vegetarian diet.

# MAYLASIA

# Beriani

1 chicken or Chicken parts
1 tbsp poppy seeds
1 clove garlic
1 cup shallots.—sliced
1 tsp. curry powder
2-3 tsp salt
2 red peppers or chili peppers
8 oz grated coconut
8 oz can coconut milk.
5 slices of ginger
4 tbsp. ghee
5 cloves
5 cm cinnamon stick
10 cashew nuts
10 almonds
1 ½ to 2 cups long-grain rice

1. Chop garlic, ginger, chili peppers, poppy seeds, cashew nuts and almonds together. Cut chicken into pieces. (Unless using pre cut parts)
2. Melt ghee in a frying pan or wok and fry cloves, cinnamon, shallots.
3. Add in the chicken pieces, 1 tsp. salt, nut and garlic ingredients. and curry powder. Stir to mix and cook covered for 10-15 minutes.
4. In a pot add the rice, coconut milk, and 3-4 cups of water.
5. When rice is almost cooked, add the chicken and integrate well. Cover and allow rice to cook over very low fire.

Note: Brown Chicken first till almost cooked.

# Char Koay Teow Fried Flat Rice Noodles

1 tsp. salt
¼ cup of oil
4 eggs
2 cloves of garlic
11 oz flat rice noodles (kway teow)
11 oz bean sprouts. washed and drained
1.4 cup soy sauce
chili sauce (optional)
2-4 of Chinese sausages (sliced thinly and fried)
2 oz chives, cut into 1-2 inches in length
4-6 oz Clams (in a can)
1-2 tbsp. sweet thick black sauce

1. Heat large wok then add oil and fry garlic for 10 seconds. Add rice noodles and bean sprouts. Add in salt water mixture and soy sauce. Stir-fry for 1/2 minute. Pre cook rice noodles. Plunge into ice water after done boiling in hot water. Or they'll stick together.
2. Add 4 tbsp. of oil in a hot frying pan. Scramble eggs in the pan. Mix scrambled eggs into noodles. Noodles of course are in plates out of the water.
3. Add chili sauce. (see below)
4. Add sausages, and stir-fry for another minute. Add clams and integrate.
5. Place the noodles in plates. Add Sausage and Clams. Add in chives, bean sprouts, and sweet thick black sauce. integrate well.

# Chili Sauce Recipe

10 oz chili pastes
1 tsp. pepper
1 1/2 tbsp. salt
12 fl oz water ]
1 tbsp. sugar
1 tbsp. oil
3/4 tsp. shrimp paste
1 cloves garlic (chopped)

1. Heat oil in a small saucepan. Fry garlic and shrimp paste till brown.
2. Add the rest. Bring to boil gently for a few minutes.

# Hae Mee Prawn Soup

2 lbs medium-sized prawns
(To be cooked ½ at a time)
¼ cup of oil
4 cups water
1 ½ lb pork ribs, cut into pieces
10 g ( 11 oz) lean pork
2 tsp salt
2 tsp sugar
1 tbsp. peppercorns
2 tbsp. light soy sauce
2 tsp dark soy sauce
1 tbsp. shallots.
16 oz bean sprouts.
12 oz Tiger Lilly buds
16 oz egg noodles
16 oz rice vermicelli
10 mint leaves

1.  Wash and drain prawns. Remove heads, de-vein and keep aside. Soak Tiger Lilly in water.
2.  Cut pork ribs into small pieces and fry in pan till brown add dark soy sauce and stir fry. Remove and place in a bowl
3.  Stir-fry prawn with 2 tbsp. oil for in heated wok till color turns pink. Set aside in a bowl for soup.
4.  Cook unshelled prawns for 2 minutes in basin with water. Remove prawns, shell and slice into halves, lengthwise.
5.  Return prawn shells to saucepan, add light soy sauce. Cook over a very high heat for 10 minutes. Reduce heat to low and let soup simmer till cooked.
6.  In a stock pot add oil and heat pork, peppercorns, shallots., tiger lilies. Add 4 cups of water. Cook till pork is done.
7.  Add egg noodles and than rice vermicelli, cook till done. Top with bean sprouts. and mint. Combine all the ingredients and serve.

# Kurma

1 1/2 lbs chicken
1 cup thick coconut milk
2 cup thin coconut milk
1/2 cup oil
4 cardamoms
2 star anise
2 red chilies
3 tsp. cinnamon
3 cloves shallots.
3 slices ginger
4 cloves garlic
4 tbsp. kurma powder (or curry powder)

1.  Blend 3 shallots. and 2 cloves garlic together. Mix with kurma powder and 1 tsp. water. Blend well into paste.
2.  Heat wok add oil the shallots and garlic paste with cinnamon, cardamom, anise, ginger until fragrant.
3.  Add the kurma powder.
4.  Brown chicken till almost done.
5.  Add to the chicken one cup of water. Cook until the Chicken is done.
4.  Pour in the thick coconut milk, bring to a near boil and pour it in the thin milk. season with salt and cook further over a low flame until the sauce is thick.

# Malaysian Stir-fried Beef with Vegetables

1 1/2 lb Flank steak
2 tsp. Cornstarch
1 tlbs Brown sugar
5 tbsp. Soy sauce
1/4 cup Peanut oil
8 oz Cauliflower florets
1 Green pepper, thinly sliced
1 Carrot, julienned
1 can Mushrooms, sliced thin
Or Asian mushroom, soak till soft then sliced.
16 oz Bean sprouts.
2 slices Ginger
2 cloves Garlic minced

1. Place the steak on a flat surface and, using a sharp knife, cut against the grain into slices about 2-in. wide. Slice each piece of steak horizontally into 2 or 3 pieces. cut into 1/4-in. strips.
2. Add the cornstarch to the steak and toss to coat. Place the steak in a bowl and sprinkle over the brown sugar and soy sauce. Set aside.
3. Heat 2 tbsp. oil in a wok or large skillet and add the cauliflower, green pepper and carrot. Cook, stirring constantly until crisp-tender.
4. Add the mushrooms and cook, stirring, about 30 sec. longer. Add the bean sprouts. and stir-fry for just a few seconds.
5. Remove the vegetables with a slotted spoon and set aside.
6. Add the remaining oil to the wok or skillet. When it is very hot, add the ginger and garlic and cook, stirring, for a few sec. Add the steak and stir fry in the wok and stirring.
7. Return the vegetables to the wok and toss quickly over high heat, then serve.

# Mee Goreng Fried Noodles-Malay/ Indian-Style

2-3 tbsp. tomato sauce
1-2 tbsp. light soy sauce
4 green chilies, sliced
4 red chilies, sliced
4 small potatoes; boiled, skinned and cut into wedges
Oil for frying
1 onion, sliced finely
2 tomatoes, cut into wedges
8 oz Bok Choy (Chinese cabbage) cut 2 in lengths
16 oz bean sprouts.
12 oz fresh yellow noodles
4 eggs
Light soy sauce
2 tbsp. shallots.
2-4 limes-cut into wedges or sliced

1. Heat work, then add oil, and fry onion slices (and chilies) till soft and translucent.
2. Add tomatoes and Bok Choy cabbage.
3. Pre cook Potatoes and Pasta
4. In a separate skillet scramble eggs with a sprinkle of light soy sauce. Mix egg and noodles in the skillet thoroughly for 3 minutes.
5. Add Noodles to wok mixture.
6. Add paste for noodles (see below) according to taste. Stir mixture over a very high heat. for 1 minute. Remove to serving plate.
7. Garnish with crispy shallots. and bean sprouts. (Sometimes, add lime wedges.)

## Paste For Noodles:

1 tbsp. sugar
1 tsp. salt
8 oz onions
2 oz dried chilies
4 cloves garlic
1 tbsp. shrimp paste
1-2 oz oil
2 oz dried anchovies
8-12 oz bean sprouts.

1.  Chop onions, chilies , garlic fine.
2.  Heat 4 fl oz oil in pan ; fry anchovies over a moderate heat till crisp. Drain and pound coarsely.
3.  In a pan, heat remaining oil. Stir fry (1.) till fragrant add shrimp paste, mix in well, and set aside.
4.  On low the heat; add the pounded anchovies. Cook for 2-3 minutes, remove to a bowl. Use as required. Store the remainder in a freezer.
5.  Top with bean sprouts. when serving.

Note:
Fry noodles over a very high to prevent the noodles from becoming soft.

# Murtabak (Meat Pockets)

Ghee
4 Eggs
1 lb plain flour
12 oz Milk or water
3/4 tsp. fine salt
1/2 tsp. pepper
1/4 tsp. baking powder

1. Mix everything together into a bowl or food processor with 12 oz of milk. Kneed into a smooth dough. Cover bowl and leave dough in refrigerator overnight.
2. Divide dough into 4 equal portions. Roll out the dough thinly on an flat surface.
3. Spread ghee on the dough. Fold and shape into balls. Cover dough with a damp cloth. Set aside for 1/2 hour.
3. Roll out each piece of dough roll into a thin rectangle/ ½ the size of Egg Roll Wrappers. Place filling evenly in center of each rectangle. Spread lightly beaten egg over meat. Wrap dough over meat to form a square. Fry in hot ghee till brown on both sides.

The Filling:

2 ½ lbs minced lamb or mutton
1/2 tsp. turmeric
1/2 tsp. salt
20 oz onions (diced)
20 cardamoms, ( seeded )
2 tbsp. roasted coriander seeds
l level tbsp. aniseed

1.  Fry the spices and onion in hot oil in a skillet or wok. Add Lamb or Mutton
    Integrating well. When almost cooked put a side to cool. Place filling in Dough. Follow instruction 3 above.

# Laksa Penang

A
1 clove garlic
10 stalks lemon grass, thinly sliced
16 oz shallots.
1 thumb-sized piece turmeric
35 pieces dried chilies
or 4 tbsp. chili paste
1 tbsp. shrimp paste

B
8 slices dried tamarind
6 heaped tbsp. sugar]
2 stalks phaeomaria (bunga kantan) cut into halves
30 stalks mint (daun kesom)
2 tbsp. salt

C
2 lb rice vermicelli
6 oz tamarind
10 pt water
2.5/2 lb fish or any varity
6 tbsp. shrimp paste, mixed into 3/4 cup warm water

1. Soak tamarind in 16 fl oz of water. Squeeze and sieve into a saucepan. Repeat 3 times with the remaining water.
2. Grind [A] to a fine paste. Boil tamarind water with [A] and [B] for 10 minutes.
3. Add in fish and let sauce simmer for 10-15 minutes (until fish is cooked).
4. Set aside fish to cool,. When cooled, flake the fish.
5. Cook C ingredients together. Place vermicelli in a bowl and mix with A and B ingredients.
5. Simmer the tamarind gravy for 1 hour. Then discard the mint and phaeomaria. Add the flaked fish into the gravy, bring to boil.

The Garnish:

## Mayalasia Garnish

15 green chilies, sliced.
2 lb cucumber,
8 oz onions
2 oz mint leaves
12 red chilies, sliced
4 oz leeks or scallions sliced thinly
1 pineapple, diced

1.  With the exception of the pineapple and cucumber, grind r
    place these ingredients or place into a blender. Chop lightly.
2.  Core the cucumber and slice it into pieces, dice the Onion.
3.  Mix these together and place on meat, rice ,or pasta.

# Satay Barbecued Beef: With Peanut Sauce

1 lb beef, chilled and cut into thin pieces
12 oz of roasted peanuts.
8 oz Tamarind Juice
1-2 tsp. sugar
10 shallots.
2 cloves garlic
1/2 tsp. turmeric powder
4 stalks lemon grass, sliced
2 slices galangal or tsp. of Galangal Powder
2 tbsp. coriander seeds
2 tsp cumin
1 tsp. dark soy sauce
1 tsp. salt
4-5 tbsp. sugar
4 tbsp. oil

1. In a food processor or blender add shallots., garlic, turmeric, lemon grass,, galangal peanuts., and coriander seeds. Add tamarind juice and sugar Blend well. Add dark soy sauce and mix briefly.
2. Rub paste mixture into the beef. Sprinkle the coriander and cumin powder over the beef and integrate thoroughly. Marinate beef for 1 hour. Thread seasoned meat on to bamboo or metal skewers.

NOTE: Beware not to do this on a stove top grill. peanuts may stick and burn into it making it a task to clean.

# Sambal Telor chili Eggs

10 hard-boiled eggs
5 oz chili paste
2 tsp. curry powder
1 level tsp. sugar
A pinch of salt
¼ cup tbsp. water
1/2 cup milk
Oil for frying

1. Shell boiled eggs and soak them in slightly salted water for 20 minutes. Dry eggs on a plate on paper towels.
2. Deep-fry the eggs in 350 F Fryer till light brown, or stir in pan till surface of eggs is slightly blistered all over. Remove to a plate.
3. In a pan, shortly fry chili paste and curry, maybe 15 seconds. Than add the rest of the ingredients and eggs. Coat well

# Rendang

1 lb meat (Chicken, beef, pork, or mutton
2 cups of Coconut Milk
1 stalk lemon grass
1 tsp. shrimp paste
3 stalk lemon grass-sliced thinly
2 cups of Coconut shredded
4 slices galangal
2 tbsp. ground cardamoms
2 tbsp. curry power
30 dried chilies
120 gms shallots.
4 B ay Leaves
1 clove garlic
2 slices ginger
1 tsp. shrimp paste

1. Slice the meat into chunks and in a hot pan add oil and fry meat till almost done. Set a side.
2. On low heat, add oil to sauce pan fry spice ingredients. and curry powder 10 seconds
3. Add the coconut milk, shrimp paste and stir till it almost boils.
4. Pour in the rest of the coconut milk and simmer until the meat is completely cooked.
5. Cook till Coconut Milk Sauce is thickened.
6. Fry shreaded Coconut till browned and stir in to Reendang.

# Bakkut Teh

1 1/2 kg pork spareribs
1 tbsp. sugar
3 tbsp. cooking oil or oil
½ tsp. pepper
2 tsp. salt
2 cloves garlic
1 tsp. Soy Bean Paste
1 tsp. dark soy sauce
1 tsp. peppercorn
1 tbsp. cinnamon
2 tsp star anise
1 1/2 Litres water
2 shallots or scallions
Chinese crispy crullers (Yu-Char-Koay)

1. Cut spareribs into small pieces and marinate with pepper and 1 tsp. salt for ½ an hour.
2. Cut the Chinese crispy crullers into ½ inch pieces.
3. Heat 2 tbsp. oil in wok. Then fry the spareribs until well-browned. Set aside for later use.
4. Slice and fry the shallots. till brown. Do not add shallots or crullers to broth.
5. In a wok, heat remaining oil. Add sugar and caramelize until light brown. Then add the garlic and soy bean paste. Stir fry for 30 seconds. Add in the spareribs, dark soy sauce, peppercorn, cinnamon, star anise and remaining salt. Continue to stir fry for another 30 seconds.
6. In a stock pot add 4 cups of beef stock and 8 cups of water. Add al the ingredients.
   Allow the stock to boil on high for 10 minutes. Then reduce the heat and allow it to simmer the meat is cooked.
7. Distribute in bowls and add fried shallots and crullers to each. If you choose, skip the boiling in stock process and have the ribs fried.

# Laksa Lemak

1 Lb Chicken Breasts
16 oz rice vermicelli
5 shallots. Peeled and sliced
1 tsp. turmeric
1 tsp. coriander
1 tsp. Ginger
1 4-8 oz can of baby shrimp
8 oz of Tofu
8 oz of Fried tofu
1 ½ cups Coconut milk
2 ½ cups of water.
8-oz Bean Sprouts
Mint Leaves

1. Bring the water to a boil and steam chicken. When cooked slice into pieces.
2. In a frying pain add oil, than spices, chicken, both tofu and coconut milk. Bring to a slight boil. Than add baby shrimp
3. Bring water to a boil a cook rice vermicelli till cooked.
4. Fry Shallot till brown.
5. Add Vermicelli to bowl and top with Chicken and sauce. Garnish with Shallots, Bean sprouts., and mint.

\* If desired add rice vermicelli during instruction to and mix well.

# Fried Prawns in Tamarind

680g (1 1/2 lbs) very small or medium prawns
7-8 oz tamarind juice
1 tsp. Sugar
1 tbsp. boiling water
1 tsp. salt
6 tbsp. cooking oil
1 8-7 oz package of shredded Coconut
1 7-8 oz can of pineapples.

1. Shell and de-vein prawns, keeping heads and tails intact.
2. Marinade prawns in tamarind juiced with sugar for 1/2 hour.
3. Heat oil and fry a prawn at a time until brown and crispy on both sides.
4. Garnish with shredded Coconut.

Note: Steep Coconut in small amount of Coconut juice.

# Enche Kabin

1 whole spring chicken, about
1½-2 lb, cut into bite-sized pieces
2 egg yolks, lightly beaten
4-6 tbsp. cornstarch
peanut or vegetable oil, for frying
Hot chili sauce, for dipping

Marinade:
½ tsp. five-spice powder
1 tsp. salt
1 tsp. sugar
1 tbsp. soy sauce
1 tbsp. oyster sauce
½ ground black pepper
1 tbsp. rice wine
3 slices of ginger
4 stalks scallions-sliced thin

1.  In a bowl or flat pan, coat chicken pieces well with marinade, allow to marinate for at least 30 mins best overnight in the refrigerator
2.  Discard ginger slices and scallions.
3.  Brush egg yolks on chicken pieces, then coat with cornstarch flour
4.  Heat peanut or vegetable oil in a wok or deep fryer (350F), when hot lower the chicken pieces a few at a time carefully.
5.  Deep-fry until golden brown and cooked, turning often to color evenly
6.  Drain on metal rack or paper towels
7.  When all the chicken pieces have been deep fried, increase heat until oil is very hot, deep fry chicken, a few at a time, for about 1 min and drain well on a metal rack or paper towels
8.  Garnish with lime slices or a fresh red chili pepper.

# Ayam Pongteh

3 lb whole chicken, cut into 10-12 pieces
or pork, cut into 2-inch chunks
5 tbsp. vegetable oil
1 tbsp. soy beans paste or Miso paste
1 tbsp. dark soy sauce
3 med potatoes, quartered
1 tbsp. sugar
2 scallions, sliced
6 small dried shitake mushrooms, soaked till soft in hot water
salt and pepper
3 onions, sliced
3 slices of ginger
5 cloves garlic
In red to be grounded

1. Using food processor or blender onion, ginger and garlic into a paste
   Heat 3 tbsp. of vegetable oil in a hot wok, add ground paste, stir-fry for about 1 min
2. Add chicken [or pork], dark soy sauce and soy beans patse or miso paste, stir-fry for about 5 minutes
3. Add 2 cups water, sugar and season with salt and pepper; bring to a boil, then reduce heat and simmer for 15-20 minutess
4. Add potatoes, scallions and dried shitake mushrooms
   Cover, simmer until chicken is cooked, potatoes are tender and the sauce thickens slightly

Many Asian dishes are served with rice. You can use rice noodles or potato starch noodles and mix in a little sesame oil or a dipping sauce. Or even rice vinegar.

# Assam Laksa Noodles in Tangy Fish Gravy

1 or 2 lbs of fish
2 lb rice noodle
3 oz tamarind juice
7 slices of tamarind
10 cups water
2-2½ lb fresh fish
3 heaped tbsp. sugar
salt and pepper
14 sprigs laksa leaves [Vietnamese mint or other variety] [
3-4 slices of ginger
½ cup lime juice
3 tbsp. shrimp paste [
6-8 garlic
5 stalks lemon grass, thinly sliced
8 oz shallots.
1 tsp turmeric
3 tbsp chili paste (optional)
1½ tbsp. dried shrimp paste
8 oz can of Pineapples
Large cucumber
:

1.  1 large cucumber, remove seeds, skin and shredded. Slice the onions finely , 8 canned pineapple chunks. 10 sprigs fresh mint leaves, discard stems. shrimp paste. Mix together in a bowl.
2.  To Prepare Gravy: Using a mortar & pestle, food processor, or blender, grind garlic, lemongrass, fresh turmeric, shallots., chili paste and belacan into a paste.
3.  Bring tamarind juice to a near boil, add ground paste, sugar, laksa leaves, ginger, dried tamarind slices, season with salt and pepper, boil rapidly for 15 min.
4.  Add whole fish, immediately reduce heat to low, simmer gently until fish is cooked, about 10 to 15 min.

5. Carefully remove the fish from stock, let fish cool, flake the fish meat, set aside
6. Simmer stock uncovered on low heat for 20-30 minutes. This should become a heavier or thickened stock. Pour on fish or add fish to gravy. Serve when done. First ingredients should be served in separate on side and used as a garnish.

Note: you can leave the fish whole and pour gravy on top.

# Belacan Clams

2½ lb fresh clams
½ cup peanut or vegetable oil
4 tbsp. or to taste, chili paste
2 tsp. belacan,
1 tbs sugar
3 limes
3-4 tbsp. water
1 tbsp. corn starch combined with 3 tbsp. water
1 small onion, sliced
5-6 shallots chopped
3 stalks lemongrass, sliced thinly

1. Using a mortar & pestle or blender, grind onion, shallots., lemongrass and galangal into a paste
2. Wash clams under cold running water, drain.
3. Heat wok or pan add oil, then add ground paste, chili paste, belacan and sugar
4. Stir-fry until quite onions are caramelized.
5. Add clams, lime juice and 3-4 tbsp. water, stir-fry well to coat Cover wok, cook briefly until clams open
6. Remove cover, add cornstarch , stir well to till corn starch thickens, add clams again and coat well.
7. Cook's Note: The type of clams used in this recipe are locally harvested on the shores of Malaysia.

NOTE Belacan , also spelled belachan or blacan are the word for dried shrimp paste in Malayasia and other Asian countries.

## Soto Ayam-Spicey Chicken Soup

1 ½ lb Chicken
1 lb shrimp
4 shallots. minced
5 cloves of garlic
2 tsp. turmeric
2 tsp. ginger powder or I
2 sliced of ginger.
Light soy sauce
4-5 Chili Peppers crushed
Bean sprouts.
1 Potatoes, sliced
1 cup of Candle Nuts or Almonds.

1.  In a Stock Pot, Add chicken, quartered. Bring to a boil, in 2 quarts of water.
    Boil till almost cooked.
2.  Add Shallots, Garlic, Ginger, shallots., light soy sauce, and turmeric.
3.  Cook till Chicken is done.
4.  Slice and peel the potatoes. In a frying pan add oil and fry till crisp.
5.  Add Soup in Bowls. Top with potatoes and bean sprouts.

# Mie Bakso-Noodle and Meat Ball Soup

1 ½ lb beef chop meat
4 tbsp. Dark Soy Sauce
½ cup cilantro chopped
8-12 oz of Asian Egg Noodles
4 Shallots Sliced
2 cloves of garlic sliced
2-4 slices of ginger
½ lb snow peas
½ lb of bok choy sliced
2 carrots shredded
5 scallions sliced
2 quarts of beef stock
2 tbsp. oil

1. Mixing, chop meat using dark soy sauce, and chopped cilantro Roll them into small meatballs.
2. Add oil to stock pot fry shallots., carrots, ginger, garlic.
3. Add Beef Stock bring to a boil. Add Egg Noodles and meat balls.
4. When Noodles and meatballs are almost done add bok choy and snow peas
5. When bok choi is soften, Soup is done.

## Rempah-Rempah=Fritters

1/2 cup rice flour
1 ½ cups water
1 lb of shrimp
8-12 oz bean sprouts
4 scallions sliced
1 tsp. Ginger powder
Or ground fresh ginger
1 tsp. Coriander
2 clove of garlic crushed
2 shallots. sliced
1 cup grated coconut
1 tsp. Baking Powder
1-2 eggs

1. Mix flour, egg,, baking powder and water and mix in a bowl or food processor.
2. Add spices, shallots, bean sprouts and shrimp process them into a paste and then add Coconut and blend well
3. Mix the batter and paste together. Than form small balls with them
4. In a Frying Pan, or deep fryer set at 350 F Add balls and cook till golden brown
5. Drain oil by placing balls on paper towels.

# Nasi Cuning-Boiled Rice

12 oz of Jasmine Rice
2 cups of chicken stock
2 tbsp. Butter, margarine or ghee
1 tsp. turmeric powder
1 tsp. coriander
1 tsp. cinnamon
1 bay leaf

1. In a pot or wok add butter, spices, and bay leaf, cook till aromatic.
2. Add Chicken stock and bring to a boil, add rice.
3. Cover till rice is cooked.

# Gule Kambang-Lamb Stew

2 ½ lbs lamb
½ cup of almonds (sliced)
1 tsp. turmeric
1 tsp. coriander
1 tsp. ginger powder, or
4 slices of ginger.
4 sliced Galangal
Or 2 tsp. Galangal
4 cloves of garlic (crushed)
1 small onion
1 tsp. brown sugar
1 tsp. tamarind juice
2 cups of water
2 cups coconut juice
3 bay leaves
2 lemon grass stalks (cut up)

1.  Cut Lamb into chunks. Blend Onion, Garlic and nutsp.p in to a paste.
2.  Heat a wok or Frying Pan, add paste, lemon grass stalks, bay leaves and spices. Fry till aromatic.
3.  Add lamb and cook till browned. Add water, tamarind juice, and sugar. Cook til lamb is done.
4.  Add coconut milk and cook till it simmers.

# Bebek Hijau-Duck in Green Chili Sauce

3 lb duck about cut in 10-12 serving pieces
2 tbsp. lime juice
1 quart of cups water
5 kaffir lime leaves
1 tsp. turmeric
2 stems lemongrass bottom
Spice paste
2 tsp black peppercorns
8 Almonds, Cashews or candlenuts
10-15 fresh green chillies sliced
4 shallots. chopped
2 tbsp. galangal
1 ½ tsp ginger
1 ½ tspf turmeric
1 tsp. salt

1. Sprinkle duck pieces with lime juice and set aside.
2. Prepare spices paste by grinding peppercorns and nuts to a powder add chilies' shallots. galangal, ginger, turmeric, and salt process until smooth adding a little water if needed to keep the mixture from sticking.
3. Heat oil in a wok and gently stir fry spice paste until fragrant about 4 to 5 minutes add the water and bring to the boil stirring put in the duck lime and turmeric lime leaves and lemongrass simmer uncovered turning the duck frequently until tender and the sauce has thickened This may take 60 to 90 minutes.

# Sambal Kelapa-Coconut Relish

12 oz Fresh coconut
1 tsp. Shrimp paste
1 clove garlic crushed
3 Red chilies crushed
pinch Salt
1 tsp. Piece of palm sugar
2 tsp. Brown sugar
1 tbsp. Tamarind juice
1 Kaffir lime crushed or
½ lime juice

1. Make a paste from Garlic, chilies, shrimp paste, sugars, tamarind juice and, lime leaves. Do not mix too loose.
2. Add the coconut, mix well and serve cold.

## Kepiting Pedas-Crabs With Peppers

1 ½ lb Crabs
4 fl oz (120 ml) peanut oil
6 shallots., chopped
4 garlic cloves, chopped
1 tsp. turmeric powder
4 slices ginger
2-4 tbsp. Light soy sauce
4-6 dried red peppers
2 tbsp. yellow bean paste
1 tsp. salt
1 tsp. sugar

1. Clean the crabs. Remove back shell and clean debris.
2. In a blender mix shallots., ginger, red peppers, yellow bean paste salt and sugar.
   Blend well till a paste is formed.
3. In A Stock Pot add oil, then the paste, stir for one minute, Add crabs and cover with water.
4. When Crabs are cooked., serve hot.

Note: Adding an Asian Beer picks up the flavor.

# Bola Bola Tahu-Bean Curd Balls

400 gr Tofu mashed
2 eggs, beaten
1 lb dried shrimp
4 stalks of scallions-chopped fine
2 tbsp corn starch
1/3 cup sesame seeds
Vegetable oil for frying
3 cloves of garlic
Salt & pepper to taste
:

1.  Mix the tofu, egg, shrimp and spring onion. Ground the spices
2.  Add the spices, corn starch and mix well.
3.  Take small amounts of the mixture and roll into small balls
4.  Roll balls in the sesame seeds
5.  Deep fry in 350F of hot oil till golden brown.

# Pais Ikan-Baked Fish

2 fish
3 shallots.
2 garlic
1 large onion
½ ginger
½ inch fresh turmeric
3 red chilies
Coriander leaf or
4 oz tamarind juice
Banana leafs
Salt

1. Blend all spice, garlic, shallots., and onions in a blender or food processor.
2. Add tamarind juice to the above ingredients. Make sure this isn't too loose. It should be slightly thick.
3. Mix thoroughly with the white fish. Wrap the fish in banana leaf (you can also use aluminum foil). Steam or grill for 20 minutes, low heat in a steamer.